Life and Death
in the United States

Life and Death in the United States

Statistics on Life Expectancies,
Diseases and Death Rates
for the Twentieth Century

RUSSELL O. WRIGHT

McFarland & Company, Inc., Publishers
Jefferson, North Carolina, and London

To Doris, Eleanor, Francis, Mary Emma, and Ruth

British Library Cataloguing-in-Publication data are available

Library of Congress Cataloguing-in-Publication data are available

ISBN 0-7864-0320-9 (sewn softcover : 55# alkaline paper)

Manufactured in the United States of America

*McFarland & Company, Inc., Publishers
Box 611, Jefferson, North Carolina 28640*

Acknowledgments

I want to thank Barbara Kar of the American Cancer Society and Nancy Haase of the American Heart Association for providing information from their respective organizations that was very helpful in preparing this book.

I also want to thank Elizabeth Jackson of the National Center for Health Statistics for taking the time and trouble to compile and provide historical data from 1900 onward regarding the leading causes of death in the United States. Not only were the data very useful, but the compilation of it eliminated untold hours of poring through material at several libraries to uncover information that would have been less useful than what she provided.

Finally, I want to thank Dr. Wojciech Jasinski for his help over the years in providing uncounted reprints from the many medical journals of the world. I also want to acknowledge our discussions many years ago in the wee small hours of the morning, when we pondered the fate of mankind and the meaning of it all. They were grist for the mill in this and my previous books.

Table of Contents

List of Figures

Part IV: Cancer

List of Tables

Preface

In February of 1963, my father died of a heart attack four months short of his 54th birthday. I had turned 27 one month earlier, and my father's premature death turned a casual interest in health and medicine into a much more serious study. It was an early step in the chain of events that led to this book.

I was aware that my father's father, and his father before him, both died of heart attacks in their 50s. I knew genetics played a strong role in heart attacks, but at the time some doctors were saying heart attacks, especially for men still in their 50s, were at "epidemic" proportions and there were steps that could be taken to help prevent them. I now had the necessary incentive to learn and follow those steps. (Part III of this book confirms that the early 1960s marked a historical peak in deaths from heart attacks, and it also confirms that for those willing to take the appropriate steps the risk could be reduced.)

In January of 1993, almost exactly 30 years after my father's death, my mother suffered a stroke on the day after my 57th birthday. Fortunately she survived, although she lost most of her ability to speak and some mobility. She was only six weeks away from her 85th birthday at the time, but she continues to live comfortably and alert today under the dedicated care of my sisters in whose homes she now stays. I am one of six children, and although I moved to the West Coast in 1971 while continuing to handle my mother's financial affairs, the rest of the family still lives close to our original home near Philadelphia. For my mother, the ancient benefit of having a large family to care for you in your old age continues to be true even in modern times.

As a result of the studies begun following my father's death, my mother's stroke, although a sad event, was less of a shock. I had learned much about life expectancies and the reasons underlying their changes during the 20th Century. I knew that at age 85 my mother was very close to the average maximum life expectancy, and I knew that the same basic cardiovascular disease process that claimed my father would likely affect my mother. Because they led greatly different lifestyles, the process caused a health crisis at greatly different ages. The sites of the crisis differed as well. The process closed an artery in my father's heart, while in my mother's case it closed one in her brain. The common factor for both was that heart disease and stroke were the major killers in the cardiovascular disease process that accounted for 42 percent of all deaths in the United States in 1993 and 54 percent in 1963.

I was able to talk intelligently to the doctor and discuss my mother's treatment and medication right after the stoke and in the following years. I knew the treatment she could get was much better than that available just a few years before, and this has contributed to the fact that she is still alive and functional in most ways at age 89, four years after her stroke. But I also knew that both her gender and her lifestyle had a great deal to do with her ability to enjoy a long life prior to her stroke--and to survive after it. I knew all of this because of the data I had gathered as a result of my studies since my father's death in 1963.

My mother's stroke led to the decision to turn these data into a book that would help other people delay until late in their lives the inevitable crisis that cardiovascular disease would cause (assuming all other disease processes had been similarly delayed). Nearly all doctors agree on the basic steps to take to delay premature death (which today can be defined as death before the 80s). I knew the steps, I had the data to back them up, and by the time of my mother's stroke I had learned how to write informative books containing statistical data in a way that made the information accessible to everyone.

I started out as an electrical engineer and moved up the management line to become an executive in the aerospace electronics business. In the 1980s I took a leave of absence from the executive suite to write a book on management that was published in 1990. But even before it was published I found I liked the process of writing books so much that I retired to do it full time (my mother and I retired in the same year--she worked a regular 40 hour week until she was nearly 80 while I gave it up just after turning 50. I have some good genes to fall back on). After 1990 I wrote two statistical histories of baseball, followed that with a statistical history of presidential elections, and then wrote a statistical history of the population growth of the United States in the 20th Century.

All of these books reflected both a personal interest in their subjects and my training from my first career. I had become an expert in doing statistical analysis with computers, but my special skill was reducing reams of computer data to concise summaries that show clearly what is happening in a way that is more easily understood. I learned that accumulating data is just a first step. The more important task is selecting the information to present and knowing how to present it. The most accessible way to present data is to do it visually in a format that permits even casual observers to grasp the key issues.

Thus, the purpose of this book is to present data on life expectancy and the key causes of death in a way that makes it possible for even a casual observer to understand how life expectancy has changed in this century, to understand the key changes in the causes of death that produced the life expectancy changes, and to learn how to delay the impact of those causes so that each person can enjoy the full complement of years available. We cannot control the maximum number of years available, but we can do much individually to reach that maximum.

The Introduction that follows explains exactly what is meant by life expectancy, and also explains why it is important to know life expectancies at different ages to fully understand their meaning and potential. It also discusses the leading causes of death in the 20th Century, explains how they are defined and grouped, and explains how and why they have changed between 1900 and 2000. Once life expectancy and the leading causes of death are known and understood, it is much easier to comprehend the steps to take to prevent premature death and to reach your full life expectancy at any age.

The book is divided into five parts. Part I shows life expectancies at various ages. It shows that although life expectancy at birth has increased by 60 percent in the 20th Century, the maximum life span did not change at all (and hasn't changed for centuries). The increase in life expectancy is due to the elimination of premature death, not an increase in the maximum life span. More people living longer will increase life expectancy at every age, but that doesn't change the maximum age to which people can live. You will be able to readily determine your personal life expectancy at any age from the tables shown in Part I.

Part II shows the leading causes of death at different times in the century. Infectious diseases of all types declined as a leading cause of death well before the general use of antibiotics in the 1940s, and even though there is much discussion today of a potential new surge in infectious diseases, they presently account for less than 10 percent of all deaths (AIDS is less than 2 percent). The three leading causes of death (heart disease, cancer, and stroke) have remained in the top three positions since 1950, and total cardiovascular diseases and cancer accounted for two-thirds of all deaths in 1992. Further, although heart disease is often claimed to be a result of the problems of "modern" living, it has been a leading killer in the United States since 1900.

Because of the major impact of cardiovascular diseases and cancer on present death rates, Parts III and IV of the book address these diseases in greater detail. Part III shows how heart disease reached "epidemic" proportions in the 1960s, but it and most other cardiovascular diseases fell sharply in subsequent decades, especially when the increased age of the population is taken into account. This is strong proof that it is possible to reduce premature death due to even the strongest killer when the proper steps are taken. One result of these changes is that the difference in overall heart disease death rates for men and women has narrowed. For example, men died of heart disease at a rate 47 percent higher than that of women in 1950. By 1990 the difference was only 6 percent.

Part IV shows how death rates due to cancer rose steadily during the century, even if adjustments are made for the aging of the population. But data by site show that except for one site, cancer deaths for both men and women have either fallen sharply or changed little since the 1930s. The exception is lung cancer. It accounts for all of the increase in overall cancer death rates.

For men, lung cancer began a sharp rise in the 1940s, and it became the leading cause of cancer deaths by a wide margin after the 1950s. For women, the increase in lung cancer came about 25 years later than for men. This matched the delay in the time it took for women to become smokers at the same rate as men. Thus, lung cancer was the leading cause of cancer deaths in women in 1990. It easily displaced breast cancer, and it reversed a 50 year decline in the total cancer death rate for women that began with a sharp reduction in uterine and stomach cancer after the 1930s. Unfortunately, lung cancer deaths are still increasing sharply in women, while the rate for men is beginning to level off.

Part V, The Future, puts the changes in life expectancy and death rates in perspective, and outlines actions to take to reduce the risk of premature death from cardiovascular diseases and cancer. After understanding the rise and fall of these diseases during the 20th Century, you will be able to confirm that the actions recommended can definitely reduce your risk of premature death from both diseases. Whatever your present age, you can increase the probability that you will reach the full life expectancy you have before you, and you will also increase the probability that you will enjoy good health on the way.

To return to my father and mother as examples, my father had a life expectancy of just over 48 years when he was born in 1909. He actually made it to nearly 54 years, although he was in poor health the last few years. When he died in 1963 his life expectancy was still another 20 years, a time he never got to realize. When my mother was born in 1908, her life expectancy was just over 51 years. At age 89, she still has a life expectancy of six years, and she was unusually healthy up to the time of her stroke at 85--almost 34 years beyond her life expectancy at birth. My mother lived many more years than my father primarily because her lifestyle was much closer to that recommended in Part V. She got to realize the benefits of such a lifestyle, and you can do the same.

Introduction

The primary source for the data in this book is *The Statistical Abstract of the United States*, which has been published by the Bureau of the Census since 1878. It is the "official" source of a wide range of data on various social, political, and economical aspects of the United States. Different definitions and assumptions related to the methods used to collect and sort data can easily lead to different results in such things as life expectancy and death rates, and thus other sources could have values different from those shown in this book. But the most widely used results are those from the *Statistical Abstract*, and except where noted its data and its definitions and assumptions are used in this book.

In Parts III and IV of the book, some data made available to the public by the American Heart Association and the American Cancer Society are used to highlight trends in death rates from cardiovascular diseases and cancer. These data are identified appropriately whenever they are used. Since all three sources mentioned do not necessarily use the same definitions when determining death rates in certain categories, it is important to note the source being used. But the fact that the data from the American Heart Association and the American Cancer Society are used primarily to highlight trends over time greatly mitigates any differences in definitions.

Part I of the book is about life expectancy. This is a common term most people recognize as a forecast of the average expected length of life at any age, and thus it is the term I have chosen to use throughout the book. Strictly speaking, the calculation of the remaining years of life is a life "expectation" because expectation is a mathematical term related to data derived using specific rules of probability. The calculation is made using "life tables" that make certain assumptions about future death rates for persons at different ages. Once again, differences in the assumptions and methods of calculation can provide different results. All life expectancy data in this book is identical to that in the *Statistical Abstract*, although the *Abstract* routinely uses the term life expectation rather than expectancy.

Life expectancy can vary with the race of the group being measured, and in the early years of the century good data are not available at all ages for all races. Thus, data in Part I for the full century are for white males and females because these are the only groups with complete data since 1900. Table 1-1 that begins Part I shows comparisons for life expectancy by gender and race.

It is important to note that life expectancy is an average. A life expectancy of 70 years at birth means that 50 percent of the people born in that year will live to be 70. A life expectancy of 15 years at age 70 means that 50 percent of the people who are 70 in that year will live to be 85, i.e., another 15 years. A life expectancy of five years at age 85 means that 50 percent of the people who are 85 years old that year will live to be 90, i.e., another five years. Life expectancy is never zero. At all ages a person has an additional life expectancy. But detailed forecasts usually are not made beyond 85 years of age.

Maximum life span is much different than life expectancy. Maximum life span is the oldest age attainable by a member of the species. For humans, the maximum life span is considered by most experts to be about 115 years. There have been many claims of people living longer than this (some much longer), but acceptable documentation of their ages is lacking. The oldest person according to *The Guinness Book of Records* is a French woman who was 121 years old and counting in early 1996. There are three others with acceptable documentation who lived beyond 115 years, and only about 25 in total who made it past 110 years. For the billions alive today, 115 years remains a likely maximum.

But the maximum age any person has managed to achieve has little relevance to individual life expectancy. The maximum life span for humans probably has not changed by any meaningful amount for centuries. Human life expectancy has not increased as a result of an increasing maximum life span. It has increased because a greater number of people live longer than they previously managed to live. Life expectancy at any age essentially adds the total number of years that probably will be lived by the group being measured, and then divides by the number of people in the group. As more people live longer, the average length of life increases and thus life expectancy increases. Life expectancy at birth is strongly dependent on deaths relatively early in life because people dying early lose a high number of years of probable life. As such deaths decline, life expectancy at birth increases substantially.

Part I shows that life expectancy at birth increased by 60 percent for men and 66 percent for women from 1900 through 2000. This reflects substantially reduced death rates from infectious diseases in the earlier years of life. Life expectancy at other ages also increased, but by smaller percentages. This is because the number of years lived by an average person increases by smaller and smaller amounts as the maximum average life expectancy is approached.

Life expectancy at age 85 increased by 1.8 percent for men and 2.9 percent for women from 1900 to 2000 (from 88.8 to 90.4 years for men and from 89.1 to 91.7 years for women). But for both men and women today, life expectancy at age 85 is forecasted to increase by only 0.1 years every five years into the next century. This indicates that the average maximum life expectancy is close to 85. This means that life expectancy at birth would not be expected to increase much beyond 85, although women may have a somewhat higher limit and will arrive at their limit much sooner than men. This makes age 85 a reasonable goal for men and women at any age today, and it suggests that "premature death" could be defined as death before the age of 85.

Part I shows a life expectancy matrix for both men and women. Based on your year of birth, you can see what your life expectancy was at any age in the past and what it will be in the future through the early decades of the next century. Each matrix is shown in terms of total life expectancy. This means that rather than giving the remaining years of life at each age as is done in most tables on life expectancy, the matrix shows the total expected years of life at each age. For example, if your life expectancy is 15 years at the age of 65, the matrix shows a life expectancy of 80 rather than an additional life expectancy of 15. This makes the table much easier to use and it makes comparisons at different ages much simpler. This total life expectancy concept is used throughout Part I.

The determination of life expectancy essentially assumes that present death rates for people at each age will continue through future years. If death rates change favorably with time, life expectancies will continue to increase. That has been the experience during the Twentieth Century, although the changes are coming in smaller and smaller increments near the end of the century. Thus, it is necessary to understand how death rates have changed during the century to fully understand the changes in life expectancy. Further, it is necessary to understand how death rates have changed to be able to take the proper steps to prevent premature death. This makes death rate changes during the Twentieth Century a key part of the book.

Part II begins by showing the leading causes of death at each decade and for specific other years from 1900 through 1993, the latest year for which complete data are available. Part II then shows comparative changes in selected groupings of the leading causes. Death rates are shown by both the number of deaths per 100,000 people and the percentage of total deaths in a specific year. Both values are needed to make appropriate comparisons over the century.

For example, by far the highest death rate for a single cause in any year in the century was the 588.5 deaths per 100,000 due to pneumonia/flu in 1918 during the global flu epidemic that year. The next highest rate was the 375.2 level reached by heart disease in 1963 (the year that my father died of his heart attack). But while the 32.5 percent of all deaths caused by pneumonia/flu in 1918 was a phenomenally high level at the time, the 39.0 percent of all deaths caused by heart disease in 1963 was little different from the average percentage for heart disease for the four decades from 1950 through 1980. The difference was due to the much lower total death rate in the later years as compared to that of 1918. The total death rate fell because deaths from infectious diseases fell much faster than the increase in deaths due to cardiovascular diseases and cancer.

The need to consider both death rates and percentage of deaths is demonstrated best by the changes in each for cardiovascular diseases and cancer from 1900 through 1993. The death rate due to cardiovascular diseases in 1992 was 366.3, while in 1900 it was 345.2. Thus, the death rate changed very little in 93 years. But the percentage of deaths caused by cardiovascular diseases in 1992 was 41.7 percent compared to 20.1 percent in 1900. This is because the total death rate in 1993 was only 879.3 compared to 1719.1 in 1900, a decrease of just under 49 percent. The death rate due to cancer increased from 64.0 in 1900 to 205.8 in 1993, a ratio of 3.2. But with the lower total death rate, the percentage of deaths caused by cancer increased from 3.7 percent to 23.4 percent, a ratio of 6.3. This means that while the death rate for cardiovascular diseases and cancer increased from 409.2 in 1900 to 572.1 in 1992, the percentage of deaths caused by the two diseases increased from 23.8 percent to 65.1 percent. It's the 65.1 percent figure that grabs our attention today.

Because of these substantial differences in the absolute death rate and the percentage of deaths caused by the major diseases during the century, Part II shows graphs for both death rates and percentage of death over the century for these diseases. This is the best way to put the changes in perspective so that the changes in the importance of the diseases is clear.

Another important consideration in understanding death rates is the manner in which the causes of death are determined. There have been a number of changes during the century in the definitions of the cause of death. These changes have been made both in terms of the specific diseases that "caused" the death when several diseases are present, and in the definitions of the diseases themselves. These changes are determined in international conferences, and the changes were definitely necessary as the understanding of disease processes improved. However, such changes clearly produce obvious difficulties in showing consistent results over time.

For example, for many years bronchitis, emphysema, asthma, and other related diseases were shown as separate entries with the other related diseases included in the broad category of "all other" diseases. Since 1980 these diseases have been grouped together as "chronic obstructive pulmonary diseases and allied conditions" or COPD. This is an important category as the population ages because these diseases are fatal primarily in older persons. But before 1980 there was no such thing as COPD, even if the underlying diseases did exist.

This kind of change is further complicated by the fact that there are literally hundreds of different codes used to identify specific diseases as causes of death. Because these codes often identify different sites of diseases rather than a substantially different kind of disease, large groupings of diseases are made to bring the total down to a manageable number. This concept of disease by site is useful in helping to understand the key causes of death.

For example, "infectious diseases" is a term that includes literally hundreds of diseases with different causes. But the prime causes can be grouped into the broad categories of bacteria, viruses, and parasites (such as worms). Treatments vary widely, but primarily drugs are the main line of attack against bacteria and parasites, while inoculation is the key to defending against viruses. The common factor of these diseases is that they are diseases caused by an outside invader "infecting" the body. If we consider them by site we can group them in an intelligent way that makes it easy to understand their rise and fall (and possible rise again) during the century.

COPD as discussed above is an attempt to group different diseases affecting one basic site--the respiratory system. Pneumonia/flu and tuberculosis are also primarily diseases of the respiratory system, but they are still listed separately because they were such big killers early in the century (pneumonia/flu is still a factor today due to the aging of the population). Continuing by site, gastritis has been used in many summaries to include diseases of the digestive tract such as diarrhea, enteritis, duodenitis, and colitis. It is used in that way in this book as well, but all of the diseases included in the general term have fallen to such low levels that gastritis as an overall total no longer appears separately.

The category "other infectious diseases" usually includes diseases such as diphtheria, typhoid, whooping cough, measles, scarlet fever, and streptococcal sore throat (this grouping is also used in this book). At one time all of these were major killers, but, as happened with gastritis, many now occur so infrequently as to be statistically insignificant. AIDS is an example of a new infectious disease that has become a large enough killer to be listed separately (even though it presently accounts for only two percent of all deaths).

If the term "infectious diseases" is defined to include all of the diseases listed above, there are (and have been) only four basic causes of death in the United States in the Twentieth Century. The first is cardiovascular disease, which has been the primary killer since 1920 and was a major killer in the years before. The second is cancer, which is now second behind cardiovascular disease, a position it has held since 1940 (as noted, cardiovascular diseases and cancer now account for 65 percent of all deaths). The third main cause is infectious diseases, which were the leading killer before 1920 due to pneumonia/flu and tuberculosis but now account for only 11 percent of all deaths. The fourth cause is "violent deaths," a category which includes accidents, suicide, and homicide. This fourth category causes about 7 percent of all deaths.

These four groups now account for about 83 percent of all deaths, and they accounted for about 75 percent in 1900. These four groups are used in the selected causes section of Part II to show how death rates varied on a broad scale in the Twentieth Century. Narrowing down the categories to these four permits a better understanding of changes in the causes of death during the century.

Another important concept is age-adjusted death rates. The death rates generally used in this book are called "raw" death rates. They are determined by dividing the number of deaths by the number of people to get a rate per 100,000 people. But as the population ages, one could argue death rates are overstated because a higher rate is expected for an older population. Age-adjusted death rates are determined by selecting a population baseline such as 1940 (which is used by the *Statistical Abstract* and the American Heart Association). Present death rates for specific age brackets are applied to the age brackets of the population in 1940. This eliminates differences over time due to age when determining whether a disease is increasing or decreasing and at what rate. This technique is most widely used in Parts III and IV of the book.

Part III shows greater detail in death rates for cardiovascular diseases, the major killer of the century. Cardiovascular diseases are diseases of the heart and circulatory system. Heart disease and stroke are widely recognized terms, but there are a number of disease processes that affect the heart, and strokes also have variable causes. Using the site concept, heart disease and stroke can be considered a listing of two specific sites (the heart and the brain) where cardiovascular disease causes death. All other deaths caused by cardiovascular disease can be grouped as "other cardiovascular diseases."

Part III uses age-adjusted death rates to demonstrate the dramatic reduction in cardiovascular disease death rates that has taken place since the 1960s. On an age-adjusted basis, the heart disease death rate has declined by over 50 percent since 1960. Raw death rates also show substantial declines in deaths in different age groups. This is strong evidence that the steps outline in Part V can reduce premature death.

Part IV shows greater detail for cancer, the second leading killer. All cancers are "malignant neoplasms," but cancers in different sites in the body have different characteristics, causes, and treatments. While it is convenient to combine all sites under the term "cancer" in death rate listings, the rise and fall of cancer during the Twentieth Century can be understood best by considering changes by site. This is the key emphasis of Part IV, and it shows that nearly all cancers in both men and women have remained nearly stable or declined sharply since the 1930s except for lung cancer. The increase in lung cancer accounts for all of the increase in the overall cancer death rate since 1930.

Part V, The Future, shows the present major killers by different age groups and forecasts their future impacts. This defines the problems that need to be addressed to take steps to eliminate or at least defer the effects of the diseases most likely to cause our death. The background gained from the previous parts of the book will help you understand how these steps can avoid premature death and permit you to reach your full potential life expectancy.

Part I
Life Expectancy

Life Expectancy at Different Ages

As discussed in the Introduction, life expectancy is an average. A life expectancy of 70 years at birth means that 50 percent of the people born that year will live to be 70. A life expectancy of 15 years at age 70 means that 50 percent of the people turning 70 that year will live to be 85, i.e., another 15 years. When most people talk about life expectancy, they mean life expectancy at birth. But the most important life expectancy for each individual is life expectancy at his or her present age. Thus, the key information needed is present life expectancy at different ages and the forecasted changes at those ages.

One of the first tables of life expectancies was published in 1693 by Edmund Halley, the man after whom Halley's Comet is named. He analyzed records from the city of Breslau and found a life expectancy at birth of 33 years and a life expectancy at age 80 of six years. Exactly 300 years later in 1993, life expectancy at birth in the United States was nearly 76 years, a gain of 43 years. But life expectancy at age 80 was less than nine years, a gain of only three years in three centuries. This is the first of many examples in this book showing that although life expectancy at birth has continually increased, life expectancy after age 80 has changed relatively little.

As explained in the Introduction, this difference is because increasing life expectancies at birth are due to the reduction of premature death (death before age 85). Once a person passes 80, there is little premature death to prevent. Since life expectancy at birth (or any age) is essentially an average of the probable number of future years people at that age will live divided by the number of people in the sample being considered, a reduction in premature death at early ages has a substantial impact on life expectancy at birth. But if the life span limit does not change over time, life expectancy at advanced ages will change very little. This is precisely what has happened since records were kept, confirming that the maximum life span has not changed.

It is estimated that life expectancy at birth in Europe was 18 or less for many centuries after humans appeared on the scene. By the time of the Roman Empire about 2000 years ago, it had climbed to about 22 years. In the middle ages it was over 30 years, and it grew to about 35 years by the time the Revolutionary War started in the United States. Over the next 125 years life expectancy at birth in the United States increased to the high 40s, reaching a level of about 47 years at our starting point of 1900.

The figures in Part I show life expectancy at birth and at different ages from 1900 through 2000. Because women have higher life expectancies than men at all ages, separate figures are shown for men and women. As explained in the Introduction, most of the data shown in Part I are for white males and females because this is the only group for which data are available for the full century at all ages. However, the trends shown are consistent for all races.

To permit a comparison of the differences in life expectancy by gender and race, Table 1-1 shows life expectancies in 1992 at various ages for the nation overall and for white and black males and females. Table 1-1 shows total life expectancy at each age rather than just the remaining years of life. This makes it easier to make comparisons at different ages for the different groups. The total life expectancy concept is used throughout Part I.

Table 1-1. Total Life Expectancy Overview

	Overall	Female		Male	
		White	Black	White	Black
At Birth	75.8	79.8	73.9	73.2	65.0
Age 20	76.9	80.6	75.6	74.3	67.2
Age 40	78.3	81.2	77.1	76.0	70.5
Age 60	81.1	83.2	80.8	79.1	76.3
Age 80	88.5	89.2	88.6	87.2	86.8
Age 85	91.2	91.6	91.3	90.3	90.1

Table 1.1 shows that gender is more important than race in determining life expectancy. A white female has the greatest life expectancy at all ages, and a black female has a greater life expectancy than both white and black males at all ages. But the differences narrow every year after birth. By age 85 the differences by race are insignificant, and the differences by gender are below 1.7 percent.

Life expectancy at birth for a white female is 14.8 years higher than that for a black male. But by age 40 a black male gains 5.5 years in life expectancy compared to 1.4 for a white female. By age 60 the difference is down to 6.9 years, and at age 85 it is only 1.5 years. By age 85 a black male gains 25.1 years over life expectancy at birth while a white female gains only 11.8 years. These differences are due to the fact that the maximum life span is basically the same for everyone. Large differences in life expectancy occur only early in life due to different death rates at younger ages for each group. The rest of Part I shows how life expectancy at different ages evolved during the Twentieth Century.

Figure 1-1 shows life expectancy in years for males at birth and at age 85 from 1900 through 2000. The exact years are shown numerically in the table under the graph. The table also shows the cumulative gain in life expectancy for each decade with 1900 as the baseline. The last column shows the difference between life expectancy at age 85 and at birth for each decade.

Life expectancy at birth increased from 46.6 years in 1900 to a forecasted 74.3 years in 2000, a gain of 27.7 years. Life expectancy at age 85 increased from 88.8 years in 1900 to a forecasted 90.4 years in 2000, a gain of only 1.6 years. Thus, an 85-year-old man in 2000 who can expect to live a little more than five years will have gained very little on his 85-year-old counterpart in 1900 who could expect to live nearly four more years. This is because life expectancy at age 85 increased by less than 2 percent during the century while life expectancy at birth increased by nearly 60 percent.

This difference in life expectancy gain is shown by the constantly decreasing years in the last column under the graph. By 2000 a man who manages to reach 85 can expect to live a total life span of only 16.1 years more than the average expected for any new baby boy born that year. The difference was 42.2 years in 1900. The fact that the years in this column steadily decrease is the most obvious evidence that death rates prior to 85 have steadily declined. As noted before, the steady increase in life expectancy at birth is not due to an increase in the life span. It is due to the reduction in "premature" deaths, i.e., deaths during the years before men reach their 80s. As the average number of years lived by each man increases, the average life expectancy at birth increases accordingly. But if the average life expectancy becomes nearly constant at a specific age, that age must be near the maximum average life span. Figure 1-1 demonstrates that the maximum cannot be much above 85 years.

As shown in Table 1-1, estimated life expectancy at birth has been increasing for centuries. There are not enough data to extend the life expectancy at 85 back over the centuries, but there's no reason to believe the result would be much different than shown in Figure 1-1. The great advances in medical technology over the centuries have mainly resulted in the reduction of premature death. Only in about the last 50 years has medical technology had an impact on the life span of men already in their 80s.

This is shown by the gain in life expectancy at age 85 increasing by 1.4 years between 1940 and 2000 after it had increased by only 0.2 years between 1900 and 1940. As shown later in Part I, the gain is forecasted to continue to grow at a rate of about 0.1 years every five years into the early decades of the next century. This slow rate of increase confirms that the maximum life span of men is essentially fixed, but the fact that it does increase means that the maximum span is a little above 85 years. Women live longer than men at every age, but they also have a similar maximum life span as shown in Figure 1-2.

Figure 1-1. Male Life Expectancy at Birth and Age 85

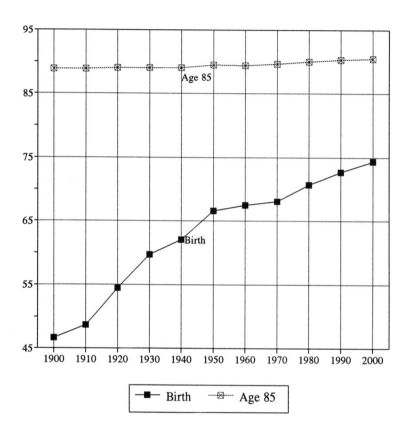

Year	Birth	Gain	Age 85	Gain	Age 85 vs Birth
1900	46.6	--	88.8	--	42.2
1910	48.6	2.0	88.8	0.0	40.2
1920	54.4	7.8	89.0	0.2	34.6
1930	59.7	13.1	89.0	0.2	29.3
1940	62.1	15.5	89.0	0.2	26.9
1950	66.5	19.9	89.4	0.6	22.9
1960	67.4	20.8	89.3	0.5	21.9
1970	68.0	21.4	89.6	0.8	21.6
1980	70.7	24.1	90.0	1.2	19.3
1990	72.7	26.1	90.2	1.4	17.5
2000	74.3	27.7	90.4	1.6	16.1

Figure 1-2 shows life expectancy in years for females at birth and at age 85 from 1900 through 2000. The exact years are shown numerically in the table under the graph. The table also shows the cumulative gain in life expectancy for each decade with 1900 as the baseline. The last column shows the difference between life expectancy at age 85 and at birth for each decade.

Life expectancy at birth increased from 48.7 years in 1900 to a forecasted 80.9 years in 2000, a gain of 32.2 years. Life expectancy at age 85 increased from 89.1 years in 1900 to a forecasted 91.7 years in 2000, a gain of only 2.6 years. Thus, an 85-year-old woman in 2000 who can expect to live a little less than seven more years will have gained less than three years on her 85-year-old counterpart in 1900 who could expect to live just over four more years. This is because life expectancy at age 85 increased by just under 3 percent during the century, while life expectancy at birth increased by over 66 percent.

This difference in life expectancy gain is shown by the constantly decreasing years in the last column under the graph. By 2000 a woman who manages to reach 85 can expect to live a total life span of only 10.8 years more than the average expected for any new baby girl born that year. The difference was 40.4 years in 1900. The fact that the years in this column steadily decrease is the most obvious evidence that death rates prior to age 85 have constantly decreased. As noted before, the steady increase in life expectancy at birth is not due to an increase in the life span. It is due to the reduction in "premature" deaths, i.e., deaths during the years before women reach their 80s. As the average number of years lived by each woman increases, the average life expectancy at birth increases accordingly. But if the average life expectancy is nearly constant at a specific age, that age must be near the maximum average life span. Figure 1-2 demonstrates that the maximum cannot be much above 85 years.

As shown in Table 1-1, estimated life expectancy at birth has been increasing for centuries. There are not enough data to extend the life expectancy at 85 back over the centuries, but there's no reason to believe the result would be much different than shown in Figure 1-1. The great advances in medical technology over the centuries have mainly resulted in the reduction of premature death. Only in about the last 50 years has medical technology had an impact on the life span of women already in their 80s.

This is shown by the gain in life expectancy at age 85 increasing by 2.4 years between 1940 and 2000 after it had increased by only 0.2 years between 1900 and 1940. As shown later in Part I, the gain is forecasted to continue to grow at a rate of about 0.1 years every five years into the early decades of the next century. This slow rate of increase confirms that the maximum life span of women is essentially fixed, but the fact that it does increase means that the maximum span is somewhat above 85 years. This effect is clearly seen in the following figures which show life expectancies at different ages.

Figure 1-2. Female Life Expectancy at Birth and Age 85

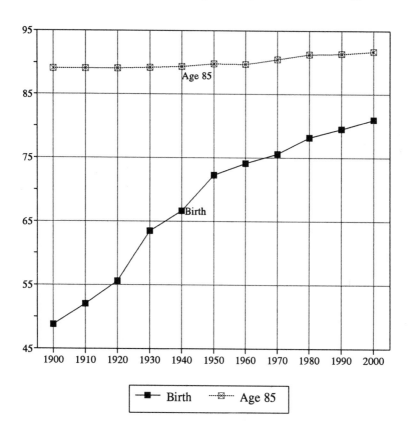

Year	Birth	Gain	Age 85	Gain	Age 85 vs Birth
1900	48.7	--	89.1	--	40.4
1910	52.0	3.3	89.1	0.0	37.1
1920	55.6	6.9	89.1	0.0	33.5
1930	63.5	14.8	89.2	0.1	25.7
1940	66.6	17.9	89.3	0.2	22.7
1950	72.2	23.5	89.8	0.7	17.6
1960	74.1	25.4	89.7	0.6	15.6
1970	75.6	26.9	90.5	1.4	14.9
1980	78.1	29.4	91.3	2.2	13.2
1990	79.4	30.7	91.4	2.3	12.0
2000	80.9	32.2	91.7	2.6	10.8

Figure 1-3 shows life expectancy in years for males from 1900 through 2000 starting at age 20 and continuing to age 80 at intervals of 20 years. The exact years are shown numerically in the table under the graph.

The increases in life expectancy during the century decrease with increasing age. At age 20, there was a steady increase in life expectancy from 1900 through 1950, as improvements in both the public health and medical fields decreased the number of premature deaths due to infectious diseases and accidents (in spite of the steady growth in vehicular accidents). Life expectancy grew by about 13 percent during the period, increasing from 61.8 in 1900 to 69.6 in 1950. There was a smaller gain of just under five percent at age 40 (from 68.0 to 71.2), and at ages 60 and 80 there was hardly any increase at all. This was because the improvements in public health and medicine had much less effect on the life expectancy of persons who had already managed to survive past age 40.

From 1950 through 1970, increases in life expectancy at any age from 20 through 80 were less than one year. Premature deaths due to infectious diseases had been reduced so far by 1950 that they were a minimal factor for these age groups. Also, steady increases in male deaths due to heart attacks were offsetting any natural gains in life expectancy due to increasingly better living conditions for most people.

But, as shown in Part II, heart attack death rates declined steadily after the 1960s. This was due partly to improved medical technology, but changes in lifestyle resulting from education about the causes of heart disease played a major part. It was an excellent example of how changes in lifestyle can produce gains in life expectancy. As a result, life expectancies for men began an upward climb again after 1970, with increases of exactly five years at age 20 and age 40 from 1970 through 2000. Life expectancy at age 60 increased by 3.5 years over the same period, while life expectancy at age 80 increased by only 1.5 years due to the effect of the fixed life span.

At age 20, life expectancy increased from 61.8 in 1900 to a forecasted 75.3 in 2000, an increase of 13.5 years or 22 percent. At age 20 the increases were 8.9 years and 13 percent, while at age 40 the increases were 5.0 years and 7 percent. At age 80 the increases were 2.3 years and 3 percent, consistent with the small increases for age 85 shown in Figure 1-1. However, the importance of actually surviving to a high age is demonstrated by the fact that a man who is 80 years old in 2000 can expect to have a total life span of 87.3 years. This is 12.0 years more than the life span expected for a man who is 20 years old in 2000. But a man who is 60 years old in 2000 can only expect a gain of 4.4 years over a man who is only 20 (79.7 years compared to 75.3 years).

Women show a different trend in life expectancy gain over the full century because of their inherent advantage over men in having much lower heart attack death rates before menopause. This effect is shown in Figure 1-4.

Figure 1-3. Male Life Expectancy at Different Ages

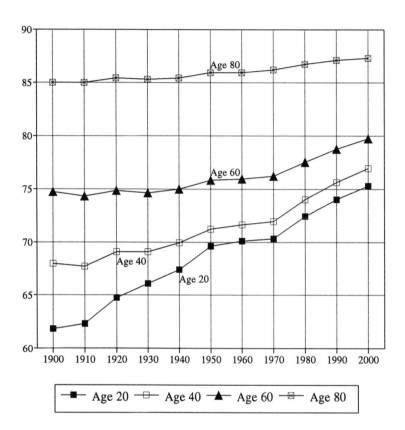

Year	Age 20	Age 40	Age 60	Age 80
1900	61.8	68.0	74.7	85.0
1910	62.3	67.7	74.3	85.0
1920	64.7	69.1	74.8	85.4
1930	66.1	69.1	74.6	85.3
1940	67.4	69.9	75.0	85.4
1950	69.6	71.2	75.8	85.9
1960	70.1	71.6	75.9	85.9
1970	70.3	71.9	76.2	86.2
1980	72.4	74.0	77.5	86.7
1990	74.0	75.6	78.7	87.1
2000	75.3	76.9	79.7	87.3

Figure 1-4 shows life expectancy in years for females from 1900 through 2000 starting at age 20 and continuing to age 80 at intervals of 20 years. The exact years are shown numerically in the table under the graph.

The increases in life expectancy during the century decrease with increasing age. At age 20, the sharpest increase in life expectancy came from 1900 through 1950, as improvements in both public health and medicine decreased the number of premature deaths due to infectious disease. Life expectancy at age 20 grew by 19 percent during the period, increasing from 62.7 in 1900 to 74.7 in 1950. There was a smaller gain of just under 10 percent at age 40 (from 69.1 to 75.7), while at age 60 the gains were 3.2 years and 4 percent. At age 80 the increase was only 0.4 years and 0.5 percent. This was because the improvements in public health and medicine had much less effect on the life expectancy of women who had already managed to survive well past age 60.

Women did not have the flat performance from 1950 through 1970 that was shown by men in Figure 1-3 for that period. This was because women did not experience the sharp increase in heart attack death rates that limited life expectancy increases for men. Women have an inherent advantage over men because they have relatively low heart disease death rates prior to menopause. The rate of increase in life expectancy for women did slow after 1950 because infectious diseases were well controlled by the 1950s, but increases in life expectancy for women continued unabated in every decade through the century.

Life expectancy increases at age 80 were greatest after 1960 due to the steady decline in heart attack death rates after the 1960s. As was the case for men, this was due partly to improved medical technology, but changes in lifestyle resulting from education about the causes of heart disease played a major part. It was an excellent example of how changes in lifestyle can produce gains in life expectancy. The increase in life expectancy for women at age 80 was only 1.1 years from 1900 through 1960, but it was 2.6 years from 1960 through 2000.

At age 20, life expectancy increased from 62.7 in 1900 to a forecasted 81.3 in 2000 (six years higher than for men), an increase of 18.6 years or 30 percent. At age 40 the increases were 12.9 years and 19 percent, while at age 60 the increases were 8.2 years and 11 percent. At age 80 the increases were 3.8 years and 4 percent, consistent with the increases for age 85 shown in Figure 1-1. However, the importance of actually surviving to a high age is demonstrated by the fact that a woman who is 80 years old in 2000 can expect to have a total life span of 89.3 years. This is 8.0 years more than the life span expected for a woman who is 20 years old in 2000. But a woman who is 60 years old in 2000 can expect a gain of only 2.0 years over a woman who is 20 years old (83.7 years compared to 81.3 years).

This concept of different life expectancy gains at different ages is shown from a new perspective in Figures 1-5 and 1-6.

Figure 1-4. Female Life Expectancy at Different Ages

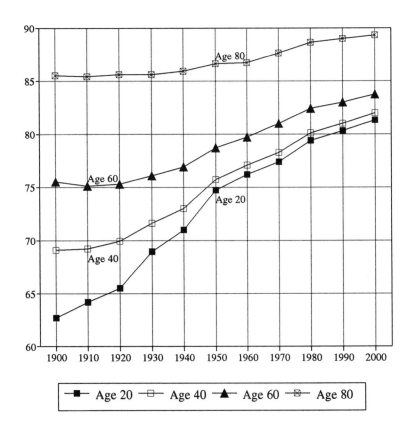

Year	Age 20	Age 40	Age 60	Age 80
1900	62.7	69.1	75.5	85.5
1910	64.2	69.2	75.1	85.4
1920	65.5	69.9	75.3	85.6
1930	68.9	71.6	76.1	85.6
1940	71.0	73.0	76.9	85.9
1950	74.7	75.7	78.7	86.6
1960	76.2	77.1	79.7	86.7
1970	77.4	78.3	81.0	87.6
1980	79.4	80.1	82.4	88.6
1990	80.3	81.0	83.0	89.0
2000	81.3	82.0	83.7	89.3

Figure 1-5 shows the gain in life expectancy in years at different ages for males from 1900 through 2000. The baseline for measuring the gains at each age is 1900. The exact years are shown numerically in the table under the graph.

The largest gain in life expectancy during the century was at birth, with a gain of 27.7 years from 1900 through 2000. This is more than twice the gain of 13.5 years at age 20 over the same period. At age 40 the gain for the century was 8.9 years, and at age 85 the gain was only 1.6 years. This means that the gains at all other ages between age 40 and age 85 fall in the bracket between 8.9 years and 1.6 years. This is additional confirmation of the limited gains in life expectancy over the century for men who were able to make it past age 40.

Of the 27.7 year gain in life expectancy at birth, 19.9 years or 72 percent of the gain came in the five decades between 1900 and 1950. The remaining five decades in the century contributed only 28 percent of the gain. This is because the death rate from infectious diseases in 1950 was only about 10 percent of the rate in 1900. As shown in Part II, much of this decline came before 1940. Although some sulfa drugs were in use in the 1930s, the 1940s were the first decade that antibiotics came into general use, partly because of World War II. Thus, the major reductions in premature deaths due to infectious diseases came from improvements in public health and nutrition rather than the introduction of new drugs. Drugs will certainly play a major role in continuing to contain infectious diseases, but the results by 1940 show once again that if we take responsibility for our own health we can increase our life expectancies with changes in lifestyle.

The graph shows the nearly flat period from 1950 through 1970 that was due to increases in the heart attack death rate as discussed in the text accompanying Figure 1-3. When the heart attack death rate fell after 1970, life expectancies for men moved up again. The gains were quite similar at birth, age 20, and age 40. From 1970 though 2000, the gain at birth was 6.3 years, while it was 5.0 years at both age 20 and age 40. This is consistent with death rate declines that occur primarily in the later years. Even the age 85 gain was 0.8 years between 1970 and 2000, compared with exactly the same gain of 0.8 years in the seven decades from 1900 through 1970. This further confirms the existence of a death rate decline at more advanced years.

Consistent with their higher life expectancies at all ages, women have higher gains than men at all ages. This is partly due to the fact that in addition to their lower death rates from heart disease prior to menopause, women have always had much lower death rates due to accidents and homicide at all ages. This means that the elimination of many premature deaths due to infectious disease, which were relatively independent of gender in their choice of victims, gave women an inherent edge in deaths due to heart disease, and an addition edge in lifestyle factors. This difference in gains for women is shown in Figure 1-6.

Figure 1-5. Male Life Expectancy Gain at Different Ages

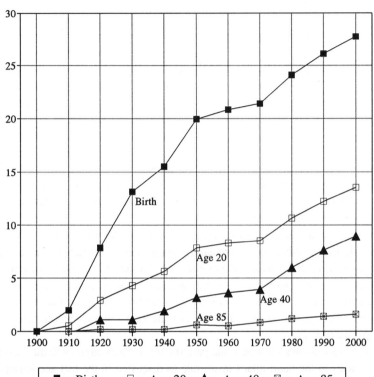

Year	Birth	Age 20	Age 40	Age 85
1900	--	--	--	--
1910	2.0	0.5	-0.3	0.0
1920	7.8	2.9	1.1	0.2
1930	13.1	4.3	1.1	0.2
1940	15.5	5.6	1.9	0.2
1950	19.9	7.8	3.2	0.6
1960	20.8	8.3	3.6	0.5
1970	21.4	8.5	3.9	0.8
1980	24.1	10.6	6.0	1.2
1990	26.1	12.2	7.6	1.4
2000	27.7	13.5	8.9	1.6

Figure 1-6 shows the gain in life expectancy in years at different ages for females from 1900 through 2000. The baseline for measuring the gains at each age is 1900. The exact years are shown numerically in the table under the graph.

The largest gain in life expectancy during the century was at birth, with a gain of 32.2 years from 1900 through 2000. This is 73 percent more than the 18.6 years gained at age 20 over the same period. At age 40 the gain for the century was 12.9 years, and at age 85 the gain was 2.6 years. The difference in gain of 12.3 years between age 40 and age 85 was 68 percent higher than the difference of 7.3 years for men (Figure 1-5). Similarly, the difference in gain between age 20 and age 40 was 6.3 years for women compared to 3.6 years for men, an increase of 75 percent for women. But the difference of 13.6 years between birth and age 20 for women was actually less than the 14.2 year difference for men. The gain in life expectancy for women during the century was more broadly shared by women at all ages than was the case for men.

But in the same way as for men, of the 32.2 year gain in life expectancy at birth for women, 23.5 years or 73 percent of the gain came in the five decades between 1900 and 1950 (for men it was 72 percent). The remaining five decades in the century contributed only 27 percent of the gain. This is because the death rate from infectious diseases in 1950 was only about 10 percent of what it was in 1900. Most of this decline came by 1940 as shown in Part II. Although some sulfa drugs were in use in the 1930s, the 1940s were the first decade that antibiotics came into general use, partly because of World War II. Thus, the major reductions in premature deaths due to infectious diseases came from improvements in public health and nutrition rather than the introduction of new drugs. Drugs will play a major role in continuing to contain infectious diseases, especially as the diseases become resistant to existing drugs. But the change between 1900 and 1940 is evidence that we can take responsibility for our own health and increase our life expectancies with changes in lifestyle.

Although the rate of increase in life expectancy gain has declined for women since 1950, the absolute gain in each decade at all ages has been remarkably similar. For example, at birth the gain in each of the five decades since 1950 was 1.9, 1.5, 2.5, 1.3, and 1.5 years. At age 40 it was 1.4, 1.2, 1.8, 0.9, and 1.0 years. Even the gain at age 85, which was only 0.6 years from 1900 through 1960, went up by 0.8 years per decade in the 1960s and 1970s, with a total gain of 2.0 years between 1960 and 2000. Life expectancies for women continue to increase at a regular rate up to the 80s, and even at age 85 each decade brings an additional gain. This is another indication that the fixed life span of women is higher than that of men.

This difference is shown more clearly in Table 1-7 which compares the life expectancy gains for men and women in the first and second parts of the century for six different ages.

Figure 1-6. Female Life Expectancy Gain at Different Ages

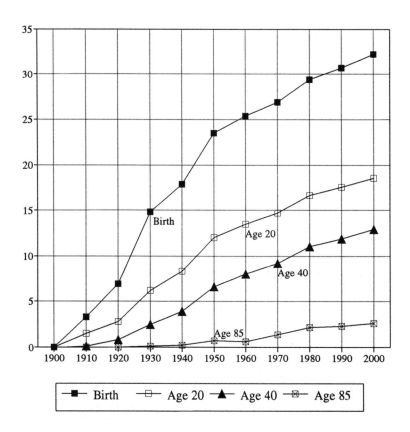

Year	Birth	Age 20	Age 40	Age 85
1900	--	--	--	--
1910	3.3	1.5	0.1	0.0
1920	6.9	2.8	0.8	0.0
1930	14.8	6.2	2.5	0.1
1940	17.9	8.3	3.9	0.2
1950	23.5	12.0	6.6	0.7
1960	25.4	13.5	8.0	0.6
1970	26.9	14.7	9.2	1.4
1980	29.4	16.7	11.0	2.2
1990	30.7	17.6	11.9	2.3
2000	32.2	18.6	12.9	2.6

Table 1-2 shows the gain in life expectancy in years at different ages for males and females from 1910 through 2000. The baseline for measuring the gains at each age is 1900, and thus the year 1900 is not shown in the table. The last two lines in the parts of the table for males and females show gains in the first half of the century compared to the second half. The last part of the full table shows the difference between the gain for females and that for males.

The largest gains are at birth and the smallest gains are at age 85, and the gains decrease with increasing age. Women show bigger gains than men at nearly all ages for all years but 1920. As shown in Part II, 1920 marked the end of the flu epidemic that peaked in 1918. With infectious diseases by far the leading cause of death, the advantage women have over men in nearly all causes of death was overwhelmed by infectious diseases, which usually are independent of gender. This effect is shown clearly when male gains are subtracted from female gains. The differences were small in 1910 (and even negative at age 80), and the differences were all negative in 1920. This means that men had bigger gains in life expectancy than women between 1900 and 1920. But this was reversed by 1930, and women had bigger gains throughout the rest of the century.

The difference in gains peaked in 1970 and declined in every decade after 1970. This means men are once again making larger gains in life expectancy than women. Women still have a substantial edge in total life expectancy, but men are slowly closing the gap. This is due to the sharp reduction since 1970 in deaths due to heart attacks (Part III). Men still have a much higher death rate from heart attacks compared to women, but men benefitted the most in terms of increased life expectancy as a result of the steady reduction in the rate.

The difference in gains also shows that the largest difference between men and women is not at birth. The largest difference comes at age 20, and even the gains at age 40 are not far behind birth. This is because men have higher death rates than women for nearly all causes of death. Thus, the reduction of premature deaths due to infectious disease makes the edge held by women in other death rates more noticeable at nearly all age levels below age 80.

Both men and women show much larger gains in life expectancy at birth from 1900 through 1950 than from 1950 through 2000. This is because the reduction of premature death due to infectious diseases took place mainly before 1950. But men show greater gains after 1950 from age 40 onward because of the reduction in heart disease that has been ongoing since 1970. For women, heart disease is a much bigger problem after menopause than before. Thus they show bigger gains in life expectancy before 1950, even past age 40. This means the advances in medical technology and education after 1950 did not have as big an effect as the elimination of premature death due to infectious disease that took place before 1950. But at age 60 this is no longer true, and women have shown greater gains after 1950 from age 60 upward.

Table 1-2. Male/Female Life Expectancy Gains Since 1900

Year	From Birth	Age 20	Age 40	Age 60	Age 80	Age 85
		Male Life Expectancy Gain, Years				
1910	2.0	0.5	-0.3	-0.4	0.0	0.0
1920	7.8	2.9	1.1	0.1	0.4	0.2
1930	13.1	4.3	1.1	-0.1	0.3	0.2
1940	15.5	5.6	1.9	0.3	0.4	0.2
1950	19.9	7.8	3.2	1.1	0.9	0.6
1960	20.8	8.3	3.6	1.2	0.9	0.5
1970	21.4	8.5	3.9	1.5	1.2	0.8
1980	24.1	10.6	6.0	2.8	1.7	1.2
1990	26.1	12.2	7.6	4.0	2.1	1.4
2000	27.7	13.5	8.9	5.0	2.3	1.6
1900-1950	19.9	7.8	3.2	1.1	0.9	0.6
1950-2000	7.8	5.7	5.7	3.9	1.4	1.0
		Female Life Expectancy Gain, Years				
1910	3.3	1.5	0.1	-0.4	-0.1	0.0
1920	6.9	2.8	0.8	-0.2	0.1	0.0
1930	14.8	6.2	2.5	0.6	0.1	0.1
1940	17.9	8.3	3.9	1.4	0.4	0.2
1950	23.5	12.0	6.6	3.2	1.1	0.7
1960	25.4	13.5	8.0	4.2	1.2	0.6
1970	26.9	14.7	9.2	5.5	2.1	1.4
1980	29.4	16.7	11.0	6.9	3.1	2.2
1990	30.7	17.6	11.9	7.5	3.5	2.3
2000	32.2	18.6	12.9	8.2	3.8	2.6
1900-1950	23.5	12.0	6.6	3.2	1.1	0.7
1950-2000	8.7	6.6	6.3	5.0	2.7	1.9
		Female Gain Minus Male Gain				
1910	1.3	1.0	0.4	0.0	-0.1	0.0
1920	-0.9	-0.1	-0.3	-0.3	-0.3	-0.2
1930	1.7	1.9	1.4	0.7	-0.2	-0.1
1940	2.4	2.7	2.0	1.1	0.0	0.0
1950	3.6	4.2	3.4	2.1	0.2	0.1
1960	4.6	5.2	4.4	3.0	0.3	0.1
1970	5.5	6.2	5.3	4.0	0.9	0.6
1980	5.3	6.1	5.0	4.1	1.4	1.0
1990	4.6	5.4	4.3	3.5	1.4	0.9
2000	4.5	5.1	4.0	3.2	1.5	1.0

Figure 1-7 shows the difference in life expectancy at birth compared to life expectancy at different ages for males from 1900 through 2000. The difference is shown in years, with the exact years listed numerically in the table under the graph. Comparing life expectancies in this manner is a good way to determine the extent to which premature deaths have been prevented at different ages.

The differences between life expectancy at all ages compared to birth declined throughout the century. This means that life expectancy at birth is growing faster than life expectancy at other ages. For example, life expectancy at age 20 in 1900 (61.8 years) was 15.2 years higher than life expectancy at birth (46.6 years). This difference will decline to 1.0 years in 2000 when life expectancy at birth will be 74.3 years and life expectancy at age 20 will be 75.3 years. This means that the causes of premature death between birth and age 20 have been dramatically reduced.

Similarly, life expectancy at age 40 in 2000 will be only 2.8 years higher than at birth, after being 21.4 years higher in 1900. This means that a man who was 40 years old in 1900 had a life expectancy (68.0 years) that was 46 percent higher than life expectancy at birth. But in 2000 a man who is 40 years old will have a life expectancy (76.9 years) that is only 3 percent higher than at birth. Once again, the causes of premature birth between birth and age 40 have been substantially reduced during the century.

Large changes also took place at higher ages. In 1900 a man who was 60 years old had a total life expectancy that was 28.1 years higher than at birth. He could expect to live to 74.7 years, an increase of 60 percent over life expectancy at birth (46.6 years). But in 2000 a man who is 60 years old can expect to live only 5.4 years longer than at birth (79.7 years compared to 74.3 years), an increase of only 7 percent over life expectancy at birth. What's equally impressive is that the difference is still declining as the causes of premature death continue to be pushed beyond 60 years.

Similarly, although a man who is age 85 in 2000 can still expect a life span that is 22 percent higher than at birth, the difference was 91 percent in 1900. This is a dramatic decline, but the 16.1 year gap in 2000 compared to the 5.4 year gap at age 60 means there are still many causes of death that have an effect between those ages. The gap between age 85 and age 60 has fallen steadily since 1940, with a sharper decline after 1970. The gap was 14.1 years (42.2 years compared to 28.1 years) in 1900, and it was still 14.0 years in 1940. It fell to 13.6 years in 1950, stayed at 13.4 years in 1960 and 1970, and then fell as heart attack deaths declined after 1970. The gap was 12.5 years in 1980, and will be 10.7 years in 2000. This means medical technology and education are having a positive effect even on men who managed to make it past the age of 85.

Figure 1-8 shows the same life expectancy measurements for women, and their results are even more impressive than those of Figure 1-9 for men.

Figure 1-7. Male Life Expectancy vs Birth at Different Ages

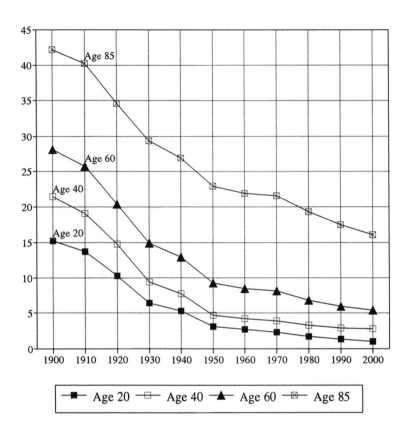

Year	Age 20	Age 40	Age 60	Age 85
1900	15.2	21.4	28.1	42.2
1910	13.7	19.1	25.7	40.2
1920	10.3	14.7	20.4	34.6
1930	6.4	9.4	14.9	29.3
1940	5.3	7.8	12.9	26.9
1950	3.1	4.7	9.3	22.9
1960	2.7	4.2	8.5	21.9
1970	2.3	3.9	8.2	21.6
1980	1.7	3.3	6.8	19.3
1990	1.3	2.9	6.0	17.5
2000	1.0	2.6	5.4	16.1

Figure 1-8 shows the difference in life expectancy at birth compared to life expectancy at different ages for females from 1900 through 2000. The difference is shown in years, with the exact years listed numerically in the table under the graph. Comparing life expectancies in this manner is a good way to determine the extent to which premature deaths have been prevented at different ages.

The differences between life expectancy at all ages compared to birth declined throughout the century. This means that life expectancy at birth is growing faster than life expectancy at other ages. For example, life expectancy at age 20 in 1900 (62.7 years) was 14.0 years higher than life expectancy at birth (48.7 years). This difference will decline to 0.4 years in 2000 when life expectancy at birth will be 80.9 years and life expectancy at age 20 will be 81.3 years. This means that the rate of premature death for women between birth and age 20 will be extremely low by 2000.

Similarly, life expectancy at age 40 in 2000 will be only 1.1 years higher than at birth, after being 20.4 years higher in 1900. This means that a woman who was 40 years old in 1900 had a life expectancy (69.1 years) that was 42 percent higher than her life expectancy at birth. But in 2000 a woman who is 40 years old will have a life expectancy (82.0 years) that is only 1 percent higher than at birth. This means the rate of premature death between birth and age 40 will also be approaching a very low level by the end of the century.

Large changes also took place at higher ages. In 1900 a woman who was 60 years old had a total life expectancy that was 26.8 years higher than at birth. She could expect to live to 75.5 years, an increase of 55 percent over life expectancy at birth (48.7 years). But in 2000 a woman who is 60 years old can expect to live only 2.8 years longer than at birth (83.7 years compared to 80.9 years), an increase of only 3 percent over life expectancy at birth. Equally impressive, the difference is still declining as the causes of premature death continue to be pushed beyond 60 years.

Similarly, although a woman who is age 85 in 2000 can still expect a life expectancy that is 13 percent higher than at birth, this is much lower than the difference of 83 percent that existed in 1900. This is a dramatic decline, but the 10.8 year gap in 2000 compared to the 2.8 year gap at age 60 means there are still many causes of death that have an effect between those ages. The gap between age 85 and age 60 has fallen steadily since 1910. It was 14.0 years (37.1 years compared to 23.1 years) in 1910, 13.1 years in 1930, 11.1 years in 1950, 9.5 years in 1970, 8.4 years in 1990, and it will be 8.0 years in 2000. This means medical technology and education are having a positive effect even on women who have already managed to make it past the age of 85.

The results of Figure 1-8 compared to those of Figure 1-7 emphasize again the advantages women have in life expectancy when compared to men at all ages. Figure 1-10 shows specific results for this comparison.

Figure 1-8. Female Life Expectancy vs Birth at Different Ages

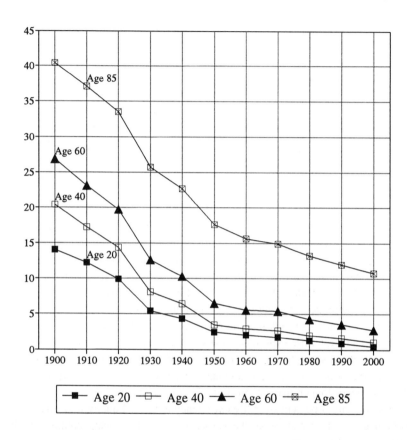

Year	Age 20	Age 40	Age 60	Age 85
1900	14.0	20.4	26.8	40.4
1910	12.2	17.2	23.1	37.1
1920	9.9	14.3	19.7	33.5
1930	5.4	8.1	12.6	25.7
1940	4.4	6.4	10.3	22.7
1950	2.5	3.5	6.5	17.6
1960	2.1	3.0	5.6	15.6
1970	1.8	2.7	5.4	14.9
1980	1.3	2.0	4.3	13.2
1990	0.9	1.6	3.6	12.0
2000	0.4	1.1	2.8	10.8

Figure 1-9 shows the difference in life expectancy for females and males from 1900 through 2000 at birth, age 40, age 60, and age 85. The life expectancies for males are subtracted from those for females, and the differences are always positive because the life expectancy for females is always greater than that for males. The differences are shown in years, with the exact years listed numerically in the table under the graph.

Although life expectancy for females was always greater than that of males, the graph shows clearly the two points in the century where the rate of change turned in favor of males. The first was 1920, when the high level of infectious deaths overwhelmed the inherent advantages in death rates women had compared to men (as discussed in the text accompanying Table 1-2). The second turning point was 1970, when the dramatic drop in heart attacks that took place after the 1960s (as described in Part III) benefitted men more than women due to the higher incidence of such deaths among men.

The change after 1970, however, was not the same for all ages. The differences in life expectancy at birth and at age 40 peaked in 1970 and declined in each successive decade. The difference at age 60 did not peak until 1980, and then declined in each successive decade. The difference at age 85 peaked in 1980 and then declined slightly in 1990, but it is forecasted to match its peak again in 2000. This continues the trend exhibited by the age 85 difference throughout the century. It has been substantially different than the trend at other ages.

As the century progressed, the difference at age 85 increased much less than the difference at other ages. In 1940, the difference stood at 0.3 years, the same as it was in 1900. This inferred that above age 85 there was little difference in life expectancy as a function of gender. But the difference grew to 0.4 years in 1950 and 1960, and then jumped to 0.9 years in 1970. This was a result of the heart attack "epidemic" of the 1960s, which had a much greater impact on men than on women. In spite of the drop in heart attacks and heart disease in general since the 1960s, the difference in life expectancy at age 85 grew to 1.3 years in 1980 and has since remained at what is the high point for the century. This suggests that as medical technology and education permit ever higher life expectancies at all ages, the inherently higher ultimate life expectancy of women over men is being uncovered.

The recent declines in the differences at other ages do not change the fact that women still have substantially higher life expectancies than men. In 2000 the difference in favor of women is forecasted to be 6.6 years at birth. This is nearly the same as it was in 1960, in spite of the declines since 1970. Similarly, the difference in 2000 at age 60 will still be higher than it was in 1960 (4.0 years compared to 3.8 years).

The data presented to this point in Part I are combined in the succeeding tables to permit readers to forecast their individual life expectancies.

Figure 1-9. Female vs Male Life Expectancy at Different Ages

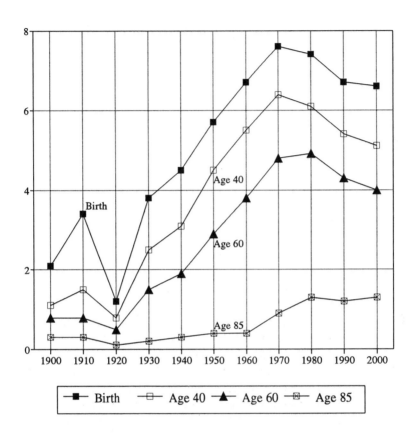

Year	Birth	Age 40	Age 60	Age 85
1900	2.1	1.1	0.8	0.3
1910	3.4	1.5	0.8	0.3
1920	1.2	0.8	0.5	0.1
1930	3.8	2.5	1.5	0.2
1940	4.5	3.1	1.9	0.3
1950	5.7	4.5	2.9	0.4
1960	6.7	5.5	3.8	0.4
1970	7.6	6.4	4.8	0.9
1980	7.4	6.1	4.9	1.3
1990	6.7	5.4	4.3	1.2
2000	6.6	5.1	4.0	1.3

Table 1-3 shows life expectancies up to age 95 for males born between 1900 and 2010. Specific values are shown every ten years for years of birth from 1900 through 1950, and every five years for years of birth from 1950 through 2010. For years of birth not shown on the table, life expectancy can be estimated from the closest year shown. The differences are very small even for years of birth that are a decade apart, and thus such estimates will give an accurate result. The series of examples that follow show how to use the table.

A man born in 1940 had a life expectancy of 62 at birth. This is the first value in the column under 1940 in the Year of Birth section. Continuing down that column, it can be determined that in 1960 (using the date in the first column), when the man was 20, he had a life expectancy of 70 years. Similarly, in 1980, at age 40, he had a life expectancy of 74 years. By 2005, when the man reaches the retirement age of 65, his life expectancy will be 81 years. When he is 70 years old in 2010, his life expectancy will be 83 years, a gain of 21 years over his life expectancy at birth. His life expectancy after 2010 can be estimated using data from other columns to predict his minimum life expectancy for older ages. The process to do this is described in the last example below.

A man born in 1900 had a life expectancy of 47 years at birth. By the time he was 40 years old in 1940, his life expectancy had improved to 70 years. By age 70 in 1970, his life expectancy was 81 years. By age 80 in 1980, his life expectancy was 87 years. By age 85 in 1985, his life expectancy was 90 years, and by age 90 in 1990 his life expectancy was 95 years. Finally, at age 95 in 1995, his life expectancy was 99 years. This is the maximum life expectancy forecasted in this table. The Department of Commerce does not forecast different life expectancies beyond 85 years. Any male 85 and older is considered to have a life expectancy of just over 5 years regardless of age. Table 1-3 follows this approach except that the maximum life expectancy is set at 99 for persons who reach age 95. This approach is explained in the footnotes under the table.

Anyone wishing to forecast life expectancy beyond the dates in the table can do so using the data from the 1900 Year of Birth column or any appropriate column containing the age of interest. If a man at 80 in 1980 could expect another 7 years of life, anyone reaching 80 in future years can expect another 7 years of life at a minimum. A similar analysis can be used for any age.

As a final example, a man born in 1965 had a life expectancy of 68 years at birth. In 1995, at age 30, his life expectancy had increased to 76 years. In 2010, when he will be 45, his life expectancy will be 78 years. In 2025 when he is 60, his life expectancy at a minimum will be 60 years plus the remaining years of life expected for a man recently reaching 60. In the first example, a man born in 1940 who reached 60 in 2000 could expect to live to be 80 years old, an additional 20 years. Thus, a man born in 1965 can expect to live a minimum of 20 more years when he reaches age 60 in 2025.

Table 1-3. Male Personal Life Expectancy

	Year of Birth							
	1900	1910	1920	1930	1940	1950	1955	1960
1900	47							
1910	61	49						
1920	65	63	54					
1930	68	66	65	60				
1940	70	69	67	67	62			
1950	73	71	70	70	69	67		
1955	74	72	71	71	70	70	67	
1960	76	73	72	71	70	70	70	67
1965	78	74	72	71	71	70	70	69
1970	81	76	73	72	71	70	70	70
1975	84	79	75	74	73	72	71	71
1980	87	81	78	75	74	73	73	72
1985	90	84	80	77	75	74	74	74
1990	95	87	82	79	77	76	75	75
1995	99[1]	90	85	81	78	77	76	76
2000	na[2]	95	87	83	80	78	78	77
2005	na[3]	99[1]	90	85	81	79	79	78
2010	na[4]	na[2]	96	88	83	80	80	79

	Year of Birth							
	1965	1970	1975	1980	1985	1990	1995	2000
1965	68							
1970	70	68						
1975	71	71	70					
1980	72	72	72	71				
1985	73	73	73	73	72			
1990	74	74	74	74	74	73		
1995	76	75	75	75	75	74	74	
2000	76	76	76	75	75	75	75	74
2005	77	77	76	76	76	76	76	75
2010	78	78	77	77	77	76	76	76

1--Maximum life expectancy for this table is set at 99. There are not enough people at age 95 and above to make an acceptable prediction of life expectancy.
2--Not applicable per note 1. The actual age is 100.
3--Not applicable per note 1. The actual age is 105.
4--Not applicable per note 1. The actual age is 110.

Table 1-4 shows life expectancies up to age 95 for females born between 1900 and 2010. Specific values are shown every ten years for years of birth from 1900 through 1950, and every five years for years of birth from 1950 through 2010. For years of birth not shown on the table, life expectancy can be estimated from the closest year shown. The differences are very small even for years of birth that are a decade apart, and thus such estimates will give an accurate result. The series of examples that follow show how to use the table.

A woman born in 1940 had a life expectancy of 67 at birth. This is the first value in the column under 1940 in the Year of Birth section. Continuing down that column, it can be seen that in 1960 (using the date in the first column), when the woman was 20, she had a life expectancy of 76 years. Similarly, in 1980, at age 40, she had a life expectancy of 80 years. By 2005, when she reaches the retirement age of 65, her life expectancy will be 85 years. When she is 70 years old in 2010, her life expectancy will be 86 years, a gain of 19 years over her life expectancy at birth. Her life expectancy after 2010 can be estimated using data from other columns to predict her minimum life expectancy for older ages. The process to do this is described in the last example below.

A woman born in 1900 had a life expectancy of 49 years at birth. By the time she was 40 years old in 1940, her life expectancy had improved to 73 years. By age 70 in 1970, her life expectancy was 84 years. By age 80 in 1980, her life expectancy was 89 years. By age 85 in 1985, her life expectancy was 91 years, and by age 90 in 1990 her life expectancy was 96 years. Finally, at age 95 in 1995, her life expectancy was 99 years. This is the maximum life expectancy forecasted in this table. The Department of Commerce does not forecast different life expectancies beyond 85 years. For now, females 85 and older are considered to have a life expectancy of 6.6 years regardless of age. Table 1-3 follows this approach except that the maximum life expectancy is set at 99 for persons who reach age 95. This approach is explained in the footnotes under the table.

Anyone wishing to forecast life expectancy beyond the dates in the table can do so using the data from the 1900 Year of Birth column or any appropriate column containing the age of interest. If a woman at 80 in 1980 could expect another 9 years of life, any woman reaching 80 in future years can expect a minimum of 9 more years of life. A similar analysis can be used for any age.

As a final example, a woman born in 1965 had a life expectancy of 75 years at birth. In 1995, at age 30, her life expectancy had increased to 81 years. In 2010, when she will be 45, her life expectancy will be 83 years. In 2025 when she is 60, her life expectancy at a minimum will be 60 years plus the remaining years of life expected for a woman recently reaching 60. In the first example, a woman born in 1940 who reached 60 in 2000 could expect to live to be 84 years old, an additional 24 years. Thus, a woman born in 1965 can expect to live a minimum of 24 more years when she reaches age 60 in 2025.

Table 1-4. Female Personal Life Expectancy

	Year of Birth							
	1900	1910	1920	1930	1940	1950	1955	1960
1900	49							
1910	63	52						
1920	66	64	56					
1930	70	69	68	64				
1940	73	72	71	70	67			
1950	77	76	75	75	74	72		
1955	78	77	76	76	76	75	74	
1960	80	78	77	77	76	76	76	74
1965	81	79	78	77	77	77	76	76
1970	84	81	79	78	78	77	77	77
1975	86	83	81	80	79	79	79	79
1980	89	85	82	81	80	80	80	79
1985	91	87	84	82	81	80	80	80
1990	96	89	85	83	82	81	81	81
1995	99[1]	92	88	85	83	82	82	81
2000	na[2]	97	89	86	84	83	82	82
2005	na[3]	99[1]	92	88	85	84	83	83
2010	na[4]	na[2]	97	90	86	84	84	83

	Year of Birth							
	1965	1970	1975	1980	1985	1990	1995	2000
1965	75							
1970	77	76						
1975	78	78	77					
1980	79	79	79	78				
1985	80	80	80	80	79			
1990	80	80	80	80	80	79		
1995	81	81	81	81	81	81	80	
2000	82	82	81	81	81	81	81	81
2005	82	82	82	82	82	82	82	82
2010	83	83	83	82	82	82	82	82

1--Maximum life expectancy for this table is set at 99. There are not enough people at age 95 and above to make an acceptable prediction of life expectancy.
2--Not applicable per note 1. The actual age is 100.
3--Not applicable per note 1. The actual age is 105.
4--Not applicable per note 1. The actual age is 110.

Table 1-5 shows life expectancies by sex, race, and age over most of a lifetime. Ages start at birth, include ages one and two, and then increase in increments of two years up to age 64. From age 65 onward, the increment is five years up to age 85. After age 85, additional years of life are shown rather than a total life expectancy. This is because, as discussed in the text accompanying Tables 1-3 and 1-4, the Department of Commerce does not forecast different life expectancies beyond 85 years. Each person, depending on sex and race, has a fixed number of expected additional years of life at all ages above age 85. These additional years are shown at the bottom of the table.

The table shows overall life expectancies for all races and both sexes, and then individual life expectancies for white and black females as well as white and black males. As discussed in the text accompanying Table 1-1, white females have the highest life expectancies at all ages followed by black females. White males are next, followed by black males. Sex is more important than race in determining life expectancy.

The difference in life expectancy between birth and age one is significant. White females and males gain 0.5 and 0.6 years respectively, while black females and males gain 1.2 years each. It takes another 25 years for a white female, for example, to gain another 0.5 years in life expectancy. Thus, gaining 0.5 years between birth and age one is significant. The other columns show similar results. This demonstrates how dangerous the first year of life is on a relative basis.

For ages up to 65, only white females show life expectancies greater than those shown in the overall column. This emphasizes the higher life expectancy of white females compared to other races and compared to males. White females represent the only category that is "above average" before age 65.

The primary purpose of Table 1-5 is to provide a reference for present life expectancies over a broad range of ages. The data in Table 1-5 are from 1992, the most recent year for which complete data are available. But life expectancy now changes very slowly with age because the primary causes of death now come at higher ages. For example, as noted above, white females gain only 0.5 years in life expectancy between ages 1 and 26. They gain another 0.5 years by age 42, and then the rate of increase slowly accelerates. But even by age 70 they have gained only 5.3 years since they were one year old. Only black males gain substantially from birth because of their higher death rates at earlier ages.

All of the data presented to this point show that age 85 is a good target for a full life. The key is knowing the steps to take to avoid the causes of premature death, with "premature" being defined as prior to age 85. Part II shows the main causes of death throughout the century, and the primary causes of death today (cardiovascular diseases and cancer) are shown in detail in Parts III and IV. Part V shows actions that have the greatest probability of delaying the effect of these causes of death past age 85. The first step in this learning process is Part II.

Table 1-5. Total Life Expectancy by Sex, Race, and Age

Age	Overall	Female		Male	
		White	Black	White	Black
Birth	75.8	79.8	73.9	73.2	65.0
1	76.4	80.3	75.1	73.8	66.2
2	76.5	80.3	75.1	73.8	66.3
4	76.5	80.3	75.2	73.9	66.4
6	76.6	80.4	75.3	73.9	66.5
8	76.6	80.4	75.3	73.9	66.5
10	76.6	80.4	75.4	74.0	66.5
12	76.6	80.4	75.4	74.0	66.6
14	76.7	80.5	75.4	74.0	66.6
16	76.7	80.5	75.5	74.1	66.7
18	76.8	80.5	75.5	74.2	66.9
20	76.9	80.6	75.6	74.3	67.2
22	77.1	80.7	75.7	74.5	67.5
24	77.2	80.7	75.8	74.6	67.8
26	77.3	80.8	75.9	74.8	68.1
28	77.4	80.8	76.0	74.9	68.4
30	77.5	80.9	76.1	75.1	68.7
32	77.7	80.9	76.3	75.2	69.0
34	77.8	81.0	76.4	75.4	69.3
36	78.0	81.1	76.6	75.6	69.7
38	78.1	81.2	76.8	75.8	70.1
40	78.3	81.2	77.1	76.0	70.5
42	78.5	81.3	77.3	76.2	70.9
44	78.7	81.5	77.6	76.4	71.4
46	78.9	81.6	77.9	76.6	71.9
48	79.1	81.7	78.2	76.8	72.4
50	79.3	81.9	78.5	77.1	73.0
52	79.6	82.1	78.8	77.4	73.5
54	79.9	82.3	79.3	77.7	74.1
56	80.3	82.6	79.7	78.1	74.8
58	80.7	82.9	80.2	78.6	75.6
60	81.1	83.2	80.8	79.1	76.3
62	81.7	83.6	81.4	79.6	77.2
64	82.2	84.0	82.0	80.2	78.1
65	82.5	84.3	82.4	80.5	78.5
70	84.2	85.6	84.3	82.4	81.0
75	86.2	87.2	86.4	84.6	83.9
80	88.5	89.2	88.6	87.2	86.8
85	91.2	91.6	91.3	90.3	90.1
85+ Add:	6.2	6.6	6.3	5.3	5.1

Part II
Death Rates

Leading Causes of Death

Figure 2-1 shows actual ("raw") and age-adjusted ("adjusted") death rates from 1900 through 1993. Because the average age of a group of people has a great effect on the average death rate, age-adjusted results are often used to compare death rates between groups (or even nations). The reference year used by the Department of Commerce to make age-adjusted calculations is 1940. Thus, the raw rate and age-adjusted rates are equal in 1940.

An age-adjusted rate assumes that the same age distribution as that of the reference year exists in the year being compared. Since the population of the United States grew steadily older as the century progressed, the age-adjusted rate is higher than the raw rate for years before 1940, and lower for years after 1940. The raw data changed relatively little after 1950, but the age-adjusted rate steadily declined. The raw rate fell by 44 percent from 1900 through 1950, tracking the reduction in deaths due to infectious diseases. The raw rate declined by only eight percent between 1950 and 1993, with a small increase between 1990 and 1993. But this is misleading because much higher death rates would be expected with an aging population. The raw rate decline in spite of the higher average age means the age-adjusted rate should have declined substantially.

The age-adjusted rates did, in fact, decline substantially as expected. They fell by 53 percent from 1900 through 1950, and they fell an additional 39 percent between 1950 and 1993. Thus, from 1900 through 1993, the age-adjusted rate fell by 71 percent. The raw rate fell by only 49 percent over the same period. Age-adjusted rates will be used often to make comparisons in Part II because this is the best way to determine true progress in the reduction of death rates for an aging population.

The results for both raw and age-adjusted rates show that substantial progress has been made in the United States in reducing deaths from all causes. These results are the driving force behind the dramatic improvements in life expectancy shown in Part I. As noted previously, increases in life expectancy are produced by decreasing death rates (especially at younger ages) rather than increasing life spans. Understanding how to increase personal life expectancy requires an understanding of the causes of death so that steps can be taken to delay the effects of these causes until late in life. This is the key to increasing personal life expectancies past the target age of 85. The understanding of death rates that is necessary to do this is provided in the rest of Part II.

Figure 2-1. Raw and Age-Adjusted Death Rates per 1,000

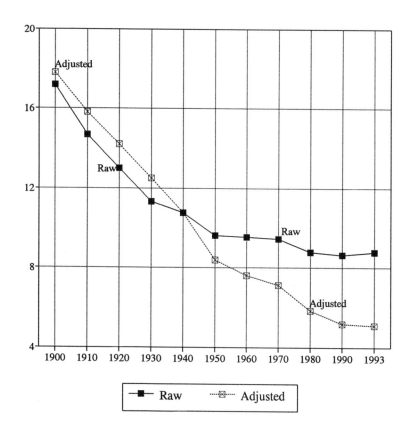

Year	Raw	Decline	Adjusted	Decline	Ratio
1900	17.2	--	17.8	--	0.97
1910	14.7	14.6%	15.8	11.2%	0.93
1920	13.0	24.4%	14.2	20.2%	0.91
1930	11.3	34.1%	12.5	29.8%	0.91
1940	10.8	37.4%	10.8	39.6%	1.00
1950	9.6	43.9%	8.4	52.8%	1.15
1960	9.6	44.4%	7.6	57.3%	1.26
1970	9.5	45.0%	7.1	59.9%	1.32
1980	8.8	48.9%	5.9	67.1%	1.50
1990	8.6	49.7%	5.2	70.8%	1.66
1993	8.8	48.9%	5.1	71.3%	1.72

Figure 2-2 shows male and female death rates per 1,000 from 1900 through 1993. The data are raw as is always the case in this book unless there is a specific note that age-adjusted data are being used. The exact rates are shown numerically in the table under the graph. The total decline in the rates since 1900 are also shown, and the ratios between the male rate and the female rate are shown in the last column.

Male death rates were higher than female death rates at every point in the century. This is as expected based on the data shown in Part I where female life expectancies were always higher than male life expectancies. But the gap between the rates varied widely throughout the century. In 1900 the rates were only 9 percent apart (ratio of 1.09), and in 1993 the rates were only 8 percent apart (ratio of 1.08). But the gap reached a peak in 1960 when the rates were 38 percent apart (ratio of 1.38).

The rates stayed relatively close together from 1900 through 1920 when the largest cause of death was infectious diseases, which are relatively independent of gender. As the death rates from infectious diseases began to fall after 1920, the inherent advantages of women over men in deaths from heart disease prior to menopause increased the gap between men and women. The gap accelerated as death rates from uterine cancer fell sharply for women after 1940 and death rates from heart disease, which affects men more strongly than women, rose. But the sharp decrease in heart attack deaths that began after the 1960s brought the rates much closer together as the century entered the 1990s.

This convergence of the death rates also brought the total decline in rates since 1900 close together. The death rate for men fell by 46.7 percent between 1900 and 1993, while it fell 46.4 percent for females. But as of 1960 the decline for men was only 37.9 percent compared to 50.9 percent for women. The decline for men exceeded that for women by 1993 because death rates for men continued to fall after 1970 while death rates for women started to rise after 1980. The result was nearly equal rates by 1993, and a greater decline for men because they started at a higher level than did women in 1900.

However, these numbers are misleading because they are raw data. One reason that death rates increased for women after 1980 is that women live longer than men and the gender distribution at higher ages is strongly biased in favor of women. As the average age of women rises, their overall death rates begin to increase even if on average they are in better health than their predecessors. If women have an inherent advantage over men in having lower heart disease death rates before menopause, then the death rates for women should have declined even more than those of men after infectious diseases became much less of a factor after 1950. Also, the ratio of death rates between men and women should be much higher in 1993 than in 1900. This is exactly the case in Figure 2-3, which uses age-adjusted death rates.

Figure 2-2. Male and Female Death Rates per 1,000

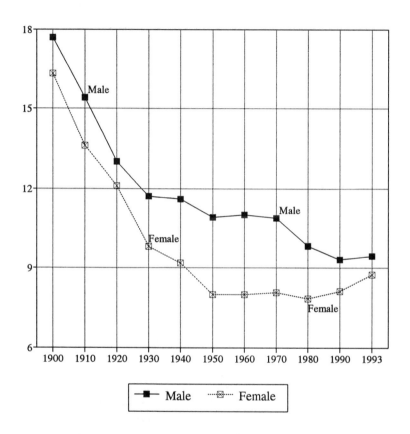

Year	Male	Decline	Female	Decline	Ratio
1900	17.7	--	16.3	--	1.09
1910	15.4	13.0%	13.6	16.6%	1.13
1920	13.0	26.6%	12.1	25.8%	1.07
1930	11.7	33.9%	9.8	39.9%	1.19
1940	11.6	34.5%	9.2	43.6%	1.26
1950	10.9	38.4%	8.0	50.9%	1.36
1960	11.0	37.9%	8.0	50.9%	1.38
1970	10.9	38.6%	8.1	50.4%	1.35
1980	9.8	44.5%	7.9	51.8%	1.25
1990	9.3	47.4%	8.1	50.2%	1.15
1993	9.4	46.7%	8.7	46.4%	1.08

Figure 2-3 shows age-adjusted male and female death rates per 1,000 from 1900 through 1993. The exact rates are shown numerically in the table under the graph. The total decline in the rates since 1900 is also shown, and the ratios between the male rate and the female rate are shown in the last column.

As was the case for the raw data shown in Figure 2-2, male age-adjusted death rates were higher than female age-adjusted death rates at every point in the century. This is consistent with the data shown in Part I where female life expectancies were always higher than male life expectancies. But instead of the gap between the rates varying widely throughout the century as was the case for raw rates, the gap generally increased during most of the century. In 1900 the rates were only ten percent apart (ratio of 1.10), but after reaching a peak of 83 percent in 1980 (the raw data ratio peaked at 38 percent in 1960, 20 years ahead of the age-adjusted ratio), the age-adjusted ratio fell only slightly to a difference of 70 percent in 1993. Thus, the difference in ratio between 1900 and 1993 was very large for the age-adjusted data (1.70 compared to 1.10), while the raw data ratios were nearly equal at opposite ends of the century.

The total declines showed a similar pattern. Males had a total decline of 65.8 percent and females 78.0 percent for the age-adjusted data, while for the raw data the males had a decline of 46.7 percent compared to 46.4 percent for females. Once again, the conclusions that would be reached from the age-adjusted data are much different from those that would be reached from the raw data.

The examples show that making comparisons between males and females (or between any different groups) requires age-adjusted as well as raw data. One way to get around this problem is to show death rates at different ages for each group being considered. Then no "age-adjustment" is required. Using raw data to show trends within a population is quite useful as long as the discussion takes into account the actual changes in the effects of different diseases as well as age changes in the population. All of these approaches are used in the rest of Part II when presenting death rate data.

Considering Figure 2-3 on its own without comparisons to other figures, the data shown demonstrate the dramatic changes in death rates in the United States during the Twentieth Century. Female death rates fell by 78.0 percent during the century, and only in the last decade has the rate shown signs of remaining constant. For males the decline was 65.8 percent, less than for females, but very substantial nevertheless. Even if the largest part of the declines came between 1900 and 1950, as the death rates from infectious diseases fell to nearly negligible levels, females added a decline of just under 17 percent from 1950 through 1993 while males added exactly 18 percent. These later declines represent the success of education and advances in medical technology in combatting heart disease and cancer. The declines would have been even greater if people had given up smoking at a greater rate.

Figure 2-3. Male/Female Age-Adjusted Death Rates per 1,000

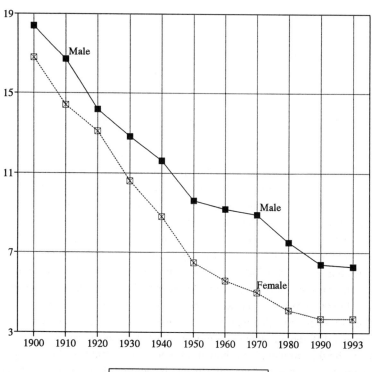

Year	Male	Decline	Female	Decline	Ratio
1900	18.4	--	16.8	--	1.10
1910	16.7	9.2%	14.4	14.3%	1.16
1920	14.2	22.8%	13.1	22.0%	1.08
1930	12.8	30.4%	10.6	36.9%	1.21
1940	11.6	37.0%	8.8	47.6%	1.32
1950	9.6	47.8%	6.5	61.3%	1.48
1960	9.2	50.0%	5.6	66.7%	1.64
1970	8.9	51.6%	5.0	70.2%	1.78
1980	7.5	59.2%	4.1	75.6%	1.83
1990	6.4	65.2%	3.7	78.0%	1.73
1993	6.3	65.8%	3.7	78.0%	1.70

Figure 2-4 shows male death rates per 1,000 from 1900 through 1993 in four age groups. The groups are: Under 1 (the most dangerous time for children); ages 5-14 (the least dangerous time for children); ages 55-64 (just before standard retirement); and age 85 up (when causes of death are no longer "premature"). The exact rates are shown numerically in the table under the graph.

The Under 1 group showed the greatest change during the century. In 1900 this group had a higher death rate than all groups except 85 up. The Under 1 group had a death rate 40 percent higher than even the 75-84 group. The great reduction in infectious diseases and improvements in public health that occurred between 1900 and 1950 drove down the death rate in the Under 1 group, but even in 1950 it was higher than the age 55-64 group. The death rate for the Under 1 group did not fall below that of the age 55-64 group until the early 1970s. After falling by 79 percent from 1900 through 1950, the death rate for the Under 1 group fell by 74 percent from its 1950 level between 1950 and 1993. This continued substantial drop can be credited to advances in medical technology and a greater educational effort for mothers of all ages.

The age 5-14 group had the lowest death rate of all groups from 1900 through 1993. This is consistent with the fact that the immune system is thought to reach a peak around age 11 and decline steadily from there. This gives maximum protection from infectious diseases and even cancer, while chronic diseases are generally not a factor at such a young age. Accidents account for 45 percent of the relatively few deaths that do occur in this group. But even though it was the group with the lowest death rate at all times throughout the century, the absolute rate declined by a factor of 12 between 1900 and 1993. This means that the rate dropped by more than 90 percent between 1900 and 1993. This is a good independent measure of the outstanding declines in death rate in the United States during the Twentieth Century.

The death rate for the Age 55-64 group declined by 48 percent between 1900 and 1993. Part V shows that the death rate for this group is very close to the overall death rate for the total population. This is confirmed by the 49 percent decline for the nation as a whole as shown in Figure 2-1. However, the decline for the group between 1900 and 1950 was 16 percent, while the 1993 rate was 38 percent below the 1950 rate. This is because the large decline in deaths from infectious diseases between 1900 and 1950 was not as important to this group as the decline in heart disease after the 1960s due to better medical technology and education about lifestyle choices.

Death rates for the 85 up group declined by 19 percent between 1900 and 1950, and 16 percent between 1950 and 1993. But most of the decline came between 1940 and 1970. The introduction of antibiotics in the 1940s and the decline of heart disease death rates in the 1960s played the major roles in producing lower death rates in the age 85 up group during the century.

Figure 2-4. Male Death Rates per 1,000 at Different Ages

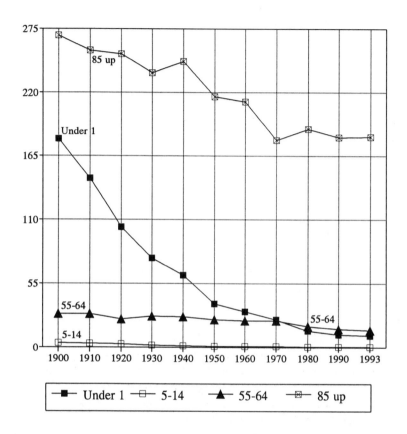

Year	Under 1	5-14	55-64	85 up
1900	179.1	3.8	28.7	268.8
1910	145.5	3.0	28.7	255.8
1920	103.6	2.8	24.6	253.0
1930	77.0	1.9	26.6	236.7
1940	61.9	1.2	26.1	246.4
1950	37.3	0.7	24.0	216.4
1960	30.6	0.6	23.1	211.9
1970	24.1	0.5	22.8	178.2
1980	14.3	0.4	18.2	188.0
1990	10.8	0.3	15.5	180.6
1993	9.7	0.3	14.8	181.0

Figure 2-5 shows female death rates per 1,000 from 1900 through 1993 in four age groups. The groups are: Under 1 (the most dangerous time for children); ages 5-14 (the least dangerous time for children); ages 55-64 (just before standard retirement); and age 85 up (when causes of death are no longer "premature"). The exact rates are shown numerically in the table under the graph. Every rate in the table is lower than the corresponding rate for males (Figure 2-4) except for that of the age 5-14 group in 1900.

The Under 1 group showed the largest decline during the century. In 1900 this group had a higher death rate than all groups except 85 up. The Under 1 group had a death rate 22 percent higher than even the 75-84 group. The great reduction in infectious diseases and improvements in public health that occurred between 1900 and 1950 drove down the death rate in the Under 1 group, but even in 1950 it was twice as high as the age 55-64 group. The death rate for the Under 1 group did not fall below that of the age 55-64 group until the late 1980s. After falling by 80 percent from 1900 through 1950, the death rate for the Under 1 group fell by 74 percent from its 1950 level between 1950 and 1993. These rates of decline are virtually identical to those for males.

The age 5-14 group had the lowest death rate of all groups from 1900 through 1993. This is consistent with the fact that the immune system is thought to reach a peak around age 11 and decline steadily from there. This gives maximum protection from infectious diseases and even cancer, while chronic diseases are generally not a factor at such a young age. But even though it was the group with the lowest death rate at all times throughout the century, the absolute rate declined by a factor of 20 between 1900 and 1993, a drop of 95 percent between 1900 and 1993. This is another indication of the outstanding declines in death rates in the United States during the Twentieth Century.

The death rate for the Age 55-64 group declined by 67 percent between 1900 and 1993. This is substantially higher than the 48 percent decline for males (Figure 2-4). The decline for the group between 1900 and 1950 was 46 percent, while the 1993 rate was 39 percent below the 1950 rate. This relatively even decline was different from the pattern for males partly because women had a big drop in uterine cancer deaths after 1940. The decline after 1950 was the same as for males and was for the same reason. Heart disease declined after the 1960s due to better medical technology and education about lifestyle choices.

Death rates for the 85 up group declined by 25 percent between 1900 and 1950, and 24 percent between 1950 and 1993. But as was the case for males, most of the decline came between 1940 and 1970. The introduction of antibiotics in the 1940s and the decline of heart disease death rates in the 1960s played major roles in producing lower death rates for both males and females. But female death rates in the age 85 up group were 20 percent below those of males in 1993 compared to only five percent below in 1900.

Figure 2-5. Female Death Rates per 1,000 at Different Ages

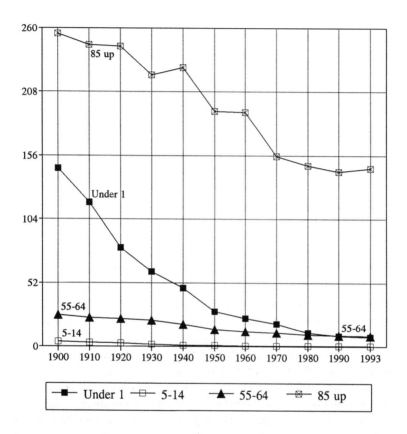

Year	Under 1	5-14	55-64	85 up
1900	145.4	3.9	25.8	255.2
1910	117.6	2.9	23.7	246.0
1920	80.7	2.5	22.4	244.7
1930	60.7	1.5	21.2	221.4
1940	47.7	0.9	18.0	227.6
1950	28.5	0.5	14.0	191.9
1960	23.2	0.4	12.0	190.9
1970	18.6	0.3	11.0	155.2
1980	11.4	0.2	9.3	147.5
1990	8.6	0.2	8.8	142.7
1993	7.3	0.2	8.6	145.1

Table 2-1 shows the ten leading causes of death from 1900 through 1940 by decade and for 1918 (a year with an unusually high number of deaths due to the global flu epidemic of 1918-19). The table shows the death rate per 100,000 and the percentage of total deaths resulting from each cause.

The major infectious diseases from 1900 through 1940 were pneumonia/flu, tuberculosis, and, up to 1930, gastritis (which combines the main infectious diseases of the digestive tract). After 1930, gastritis is included in the broad term "other infectious diseases," which includes the familiar diseases shown in the first footnote. The four broad causes of death from 1900 through 1940 were infectious diseases, cardiovascular diseases, cancer, and accidents. The other major cause, "perinatal," includes certain diseases originating in the perinatal period which only affect infants as indicated in footnote four.

Pneumonia/flu and tuberculosis were at the top in 1900, with heart disease fifth and cancer ninth. Heart disease rose to first by 1910 and remained there until the flu epidemic of 1918-19 killed 558.5 people per 100,000 in 1918 (the 558.5 rate is by far the highest death rate of the century for a single cause). The residual effect of the epidemic left pneumonia/flu at the top in 1920, with tuberculosis third in 1910, 1918, and 1920 (it was in first place six times before 1910). This made infectious diseases the top killers through 1920.

Improved public health actions in sanitation, nutrition, and health care drove infectious diseases down the list well before the general use of antibiotics in the 1940s. By 1940 pneumonia/flu was sixth and tuberculosis eighth. Their combined death rate was 116.2, down 71 percent from a combined rate of 396.6 in 1900. Total infectious diseases on the list fell by 76 percent over the same period.

Heart disease reclaimed the top spot in 1921 and never relinquished it again. Thus, it was at the top in 1930 with other cardiovascular diseases second and cancer fourth. By 1940, cancer was second with stroke in fourth place. Heart disease and cancer have remained first and second since 1940 (stroke was third in 1950 and these three have not changed position since; see Table 2-2).

Except for 1918 and 1920, heart disease was the only top cause to account for substantially more than 10 percent of all deaths. The top cause accounted for only a little more than 10 percent in 1900 and 1910, jumped to a then phenomenal 32.5 percent in 1918 at the peak of the flu epidemic, and fell to 16.0 percent as the epidemic ebbed in 1920. But heart disease caused 18.9 percent of all deaths in 1930 and 27.2 percent in 1940. It rose to over 38 percent from 1960 through 1980 (Table 2-2) as it caused an "epidemic" of its own. In spite of the perhaps greater notoriety of infectious diseases in the early part of the century, heart disease has been a great killer in the United States for over 100 years.

Diabetes made the list in 1940 because the decline of infectious disease causes reduced the rate needed to make the top ten list. This effect became even more pronounced after 1940 as shown in Table 2-2.

Table 2-1. Ten Leading Causes of Death 1900-1940

Cause of Death	Rate	% of Total	Cause of Death	Rate	% of Total
1900			**1910**		
Pneumonia/Flu	202.2	11.8%	Heart Disease	158.9	10.8%
Tuberculosis	194.4	11.3%	Pneumonia/Flu	155.9	10.6%
Other Infectious[1]	186.7	10.9%	Tuberculosis	153.8	10.5%
Gastritis[2]	142.7	8.3%	Other Infectious	147.5	10.0%
Heart Disease	137.4	8.0%	Other CVD	117.2	8.0%
Stroke	106.9	6.2%	Gastritis	115.4	7.9%
Other CVD[3]	100.9	5.9%	Stroke	95.8	6.5%
Accidents	72.3	4.2%	Accidents	84.2	5.7%
Cancer	64.0	3.7%	Cancer	76.2	5.2%
Perinatal[4]	62.6	3.6%	Perinatal	73.0	5.0%
1918			**1920**		
Pneumonia/Flu	588.5	32.5%	Pneumonia/Flu	207.3	16.0%
Heart Disease	171.6	9.5%	Heart Disease	159.6	12.3%
Tuberculosis	149.8	8.3%	Tuberculosis	113.1	8.7%
Other CVD	121.4	6.7%	Other CVD	112.3	8.6%
Other Infectious	116.9	6.5%	Other Infectious	103.0	7.9%
Stroke	94.0	5.2%	Stroke	93.0	7.2%
Accidents	81.5	4.5%	Cancer	83.4	6.4%
Cancer	80.8	4.5%	Accidents	70.0	5.4%
Gastritis	75.2	4.0%	Perinatal	69.2	5.3%
Perinatal	70.0	3.9%	Gastritis	53.7	4.1%
1930			**1940**		
Heart Disease	214.2	18.9%	Heart Disease	292.5	27.2%
Other CVD	111.2	9.8%	Cancer	120.3	11.2%
Pneumonia/Flu	102.5	9.1%	Other CVD	102.3	9.5%
Cancer	97.4	8.6%	Stroke	90.9	8.4%
Stroke	89.0	7.9%	Accidents	73.2	6.8%
Accidents	79.8	7.0%	Pneumonia/Flu	70.3	6.5%
Tuberculosis	71.1	6.3%	Other Infectious	55.6	5.2%
Other Infectious	59.5	5.3%	Tuberculosis	45.9	4.3%
Perinatal	49.6	4.4%	Perinatal	39.2	3.6%
Gastritis	26.0	2.3%	Diabetes	26.6	2.5%

1--Other infectious includes respiratory infections, syphilis, acute nephritis, diphtheria, typhoid, whooping cough, measles, scarlet fever, streptococcal sore throat, and (after 1930) gastritis.
2--Gastritis includes diarrhea, enteritis, and colitis.
3--Other CVD includes all cardiovascular diseases other than heart disease and stroke.
4--Perinatal problems originate between the 28th week of pregnancy and 28 days after birth.

Table 2-2 shows the ten leading causes of death from 1950 through 1990 by decade, with 1993 being the last year for which complete data is available. The table shows the death rate per 100,000 and the percentage of total deaths resulting from each cause.

Heart disease, cancer, stroke, and accidents, in that order, occupy the top four places on each list from 1950 through 1990. In 1993 chronic obstructive pulmonary diseases (COPD) replaced accidents in fourth place. There were more changes farther down the lists because the top four causes accounted for such a high percentage of total deaths that other items had relatively small percentages. Thus, a small change from decade to decade would result in different causes either just falling off the list or just getting on the list.

Heart disease accounted for a nearly constant percentage of deaths from 1950 through 1980 (37.0, 38.7, 38.3, and 38.3 percent respectively). The percentages declined to 33.5 percent in 1990 and 32.6 percent in 1993. But the absolute death rate fell from a peak of 369.0 in 1960 to 286.9 in 1993, a drop of 22 percent. The rate is still falling today. It's an excellent example of how changes in lifestyle can affect death rates.

The changes in death rates for cancer also serve as an excellent example of how changes in lifestyle can affect death rates, but this time the relationship has negative results. The death rate for cancer increased steadily from 1950 through 1993, and the percentage of total deaths accounted for by cancer increased from 14.4 percent in 1950 to 23.4 percent in 1993. This is an increase of 63 percent. As shown in Part IV, the total increase is due to increases in lung cancer. For both men and women, cancer death rates since 1950 have declined (sometimes substantially) or remained nearly the same for all sites in the body except for the lungs and related throat area. For men, the age-adjusted death rate for lung cancer began to slow near the end of the century, but the increase in smoking by women after 1950 is now producing dramatic increases in lung cancer. Breast cancer gets more publicity, but lung cancer kills more women.

The result is that heart disease and cancer far outweigh all other causes of death. In 1950 they combined for 51.5 percent of all deaths, and in 1993 they combined for 56.0 percent of all deaths. The 1993 level is at least below the peak of 59.2 percent in 1980, but all of the decline can be credited to the decline in heart disease. No other cause of death comes close to these two. Stroke, in third place in 1993 (as it has been since 1950), accounted for only 6.6 percent of all deaths. Even the "epidemic" of HIV/AIDS accounted for only 1.6 percent of all deaths in 1993. The relative importance of other causes of death is quite different for different age groups (Part V), but on an overall basis the overwhelming causes of death in the United States are heart disease and cancer. Other causes may have higher rates of increase, but it will be a long time for they account for a significant portion of deaths in this country.

Table 2-2. Ten Leading Causes of Death 1950-1993

Cause of Death	Rate	% of Total	Cause of Death	Rate	% of Total
1950			**1960**		
Heart Disease	356.8	37.0%	Heart Disease	369.0	38.7%
Cancer	139.8	14.5%	Cancer	149.2	15.6%
Stroke	104.0	10.8%	Stroke	108.0	11.3%
Accidents	60.6	6.3%	Accidents	52.3	5.5%
Perinatal[1]	40.5	4.2%	Other CVD	38.1	4.0%
Other CVD[2]	33.6	3.5%	Perinatal	37.4	3.9%
Pneumonia/Flu	31.3	3.2%	Pneumonia/Flu	37.3	3.9%
Other Infectious[3]	30.8	3.2%	Other Infectious	32.2	3.4%
Tuberculosis	22.5	2.3%	Diabetes	16.7	1.7%
Diabetes	16.2	1.7%	Congenital[4]	12.2	1.3%
1970			**1980**		
Heart Disease	362.0	38.3%	Heart Disease	336.0	38.3%
Cancer	162.8	17.2%	Cancer	183.9	20.9%
Stroke	101.9	10.8%	Stroke	75.1	8.6%
Accidents	56.4	6.0%	Accidents	46.7	5.3%
Other CVD	32.1	3.4%	Other CVD	25.3	2.9%
Pneumonia/Flu	30.9	3.3%	COPD	24.7	2.9%
Perinatal	21.3	2.3%	Pneumonia/Flu	24.1	2.7%
Diabetes	18.9	2.0%	Diabetes	15.4	1.8%
Liver Disease	15.5	1.6%	Liver Disease	13.5	1.5%
COPD[5]	15.2	1.6%	Suicide	11.9	1.4%
1990			**1993**		
Heart Disease	289.5	33.5%	Heart Disease	286.9	32.6%
Cancer	203.2	23.5%	Cancer	205.8	23.4%
Stroke	57.9	6.7%	Stroke	58.1	6.6%
Accidents	37.0	4.3%	COPD	39.2	4.5%
COPD	34.9	4.0%	Accidents	34.4	3.9%
Pneumonia/Flu	32.0	3.7%	Pneumonia/Flu	31.7	3.6%
Other CVD	20.9	2.4%	Diabetes	21.4	2.4%
Diabetes	19.2	2.2%	Other CVD	21.3	2.4%
Other Infectious	15.2	1.8%	HIV/AIDS	13.8	1.6%
Suicide	12.4	1.4%	Suicide	12.1	1.4%

1--Perinatal problems originate between the 28th week of pregnancy and 28 days after birth.
2--Other CVD includes all cardiovascular diseases other than heart disease and stroke.
3--Other infectious includes all diseases shown in Table 2-1. In 1990 it also includes HIV/AIDS.
4--Congenital deaths are due to malformations and anomalies present at birth.
5--COPD (chronic obstructive pulmonary diseases) includes bronchitis, emphysema, and asthma.

Table 2-3 shows the ten leading causes of death for 1900, 1918, 1940, 1960, 1980, and 1993. This is approximately every 20 years during the century, with 1918 being selected because of the global flu epidemic of 1918, and 1993 being the most recent year for which complete data is available. Table 2-3 supplements Tables 2-1 and 2-2 by permitting the changes over the full century to be compared on one page. This gives added perspective to the manner in which the leading causes of death changed from the beginning of the century to the end.

Infectious diseases were the primary cause of death for the first two decades of the century. Pneumonia/Flu tops the two lists shown at the top of the page with tuberculosis and other infectious diseases not far behind. The total infectious diseases shown in the lists accounted for 42.2 percent of all deaths in 1900 and 51.2 percent in 1918. The 1918 percentage was the peak for infectious diseases in the century, and by the early 1920s infectious diseases were no longer the leading cause of death in the United States.

The first time heart disease and cancer appeared in the top two positions of the lists in Tables 2-1 and 2-2 was 1940. These two diseases accounted for 38.4 percent of all deaths in 1940, but total cardiovascular diseases (heart disease, stroke, and other cardiovascular diseases) accounted for 45.1 percent. By 1960 total cardiovascular diseases accounted for 54.0 percent of all deaths, topping the 51.2 percent for infectious diseases in 1918. Cardiovascular diseases were at their peak in 1960, and together with cancer they accounted for 69.6 percent of all deaths that year.

By 1980 cardiovascular diseases had declined to 49.8 percent of all deaths, but the combination of cardiovascular diseases and cancer accounted for 70.7 percent of all deaths. For the lists shown in Tables 2-1 and 2-2, 1980 was the peak year for deaths due to the combination of cardiovascular diseases and cancer. In 1993 total cardiovascular diseases fell to 41.6 percent of all deaths, and the combination of cancer and cardiovascular diseases fell to 65.0 percent of all deaths. This decline came in spite of the 12 percent increase in the percentage of deaths caused by cancer between 1980 and 1993.

Accidents were the next leading cause of death during the century behind cardiovascular diseases, infectious diseases, and cancer. In spite of the increasing toll of motor vehicle deaths during the century, accidents peaked in terms of percentage of total deaths at 7.0 percent in 1930 (Table 2-1). They were close to this peak at 6.8 percent in 1940, but by 1993 they accounted for only 3.9 percent of all deaths, a decline of 44 percent from the 7.0 percent peak in 1930. The United States has consistently become a safer place to work and play since 1930, in spite of the dramatically higher number of cars and trucks on the road.

Grouping the major causes of death into four categories (cardiovascular diseases, infectious diseases, cancer, and accidents) provides a good transition to Figure 2-6, which shows these categories in graph form.

Table 2-3. Ten Leading Causes of Death 1900-1993

Cause of Death	Rate	% of Total	Cause of Death	Rate	% of Total
1900			**1918**		
Pneumonia/Flu	202.2	11.8%	Pneumonia/Flu	588.5	32.5%
Tuberculosis	194.4	11.3%	Heart Disease	171.6	9.5%
Other Infectious[1]	186.7	10.9%	Tuberculosis	149.8	8.3%
Gastritis[1]	142.7	8.3%	Other CVD	121.4	6.7%
Heart Disease	137.4	8.0%	Other Infectious	116.9	6.5%
Stroke	106.9	6.2%	Stroke	94.0	5.2%
Other CVD[2]	100.9	5.9%	Accidents	81.5	4.5%
Accidents	72.3	4.2%	Cancer	80.8	4.5%
Cancer	64.0	3.7%	Gastritis	75.2	4.0%
Perinatal[3]	62.6	3.6%	Perinatal	70.0	3.9%
1940			**1960**		
Heart Disease	292.5	27.2%	Heart Disease	369.0	38.7%
Cancer	120.3	11.2%	Cancer	149.2	15.6%
Other CVD	102.3	9.5%	Stroke	108.0	11.3%
Stroke	90.9	8.4%	Accidents	52.3	5.5%
Accidents	73.2	6.8%	Other CVD	38.1	4.0%
Pneumonia/Flu	70.3	6.5%	Perinatal	37.4	3.9%
Other Infectious	55.6	5.2%	Pneumonia/Flu	37.3	3.9%
Tuberculosis	45.9	4.3%	Other Infectious	32.2	3.4%
Perinatal	39.2	3.6%	Diabetes	16.7	1.7%
Diabetes	26.6	2.5%	Congenital[4]	12.2	1.3%
1980			**1993**		
Heart Disease	336.0	38.3%	Heart Disease	286.9	32.6%
Cancer	183.9	20.9%	Cancer	205.8	23.4%
Stroke	75.1	8.6%	Stroke	58.1	6.6%
Accidents	46.7	5.3%	COPD	39.2	4.5%
Other CVD	25.3	2.9%	Accidents	34.4	3.9%
COPD[5]	24.7	2.9%	Pneumonia/Flu	31.7	3.6%
Pneumonia/Flu	24.1	2.7%	Diabetes	21.4	2.4%
Diabetes	15.4	1.8%	Other CVD	21.3	2.4%
Liver Disease	13.5	1.5%	HIV/AIDS	13.8	1.6%
Suicide	11.9	1.4%	Suicide	12.1	1.4%

1--Other infectious and gastritis are explained in Table 2-1.
2--Other CVD includes all cardiovascular diseases other than heart disease and stroke.
3--Perinatal problems originate between the 28th week of pregnancy and 28 days after birth.
4--Congenital deaths are due to malformations and anomalies present at birth.
5--COPD (chronic obstructive pulmonary diseases) includes bronchitis, emphysema, and asthma.

Figure 2-6 shows death rates for groups of causes that accounted for most deaths from 1900 through 1993. The groups are cardiovascular diseases (CVD), infectious diseases, cancer, and violent deaths. The exact death rates are shown numerically under the graph. Cardiovascular diseases include heart disease, stroke, and other cardiovascular diseases. Infectious diseases include pneumonia/flu, tuberculosis, chronic obstructive pulmonary diseases (COPD), and the other infectious diseases identified in Tables 2-1, 2-2, and 2-3. The "other" category encompasses nearly every infectious disease known to the general public, including HIV/AIDS. The violent group includes accidents of all types, suicide, and homicide.

Infectious diseases were the leading cause of death from 1900 through the early 1920s. They had a death rate more than twice as high as cardiovascular diseases in 1900, and even in 1920 their rate was 31 percent higher than that of cardiovascular diseases. But by 1930 cardiovascular diseases had a death rate 60 percent higher than that of infectious diseases, and in 1960 the death rate for cardiovascular diseases was 7.4 times as high as that of infectious diseases. From 1960 through 1993 the cardiovascular disease death rate fell by 29 percent, while the rate for infectious diseases increased by 68 percent between 1980 and 1993. In spite of these opposing trends, the death rate for cardiovascular diseases was still four times as high as that of infectious diseases in 1993.

Cancer had the lowest death rate of the four groups in 1900, and the death rate for cancer did not catch up to the death rate for violent deaths until the early 1930s. Cancer moved into second place in the middle of the 1940s when its death rate passed that of infectious diseases. Cancer was continuing a constant upward climb at the time, while the infectious disease death rate was falling sharply. In 1950 the death rate for cancer was 65 percent higher than the rate for infectious diseases, and 81 percent higher than the rate for violent deaths. The death rate for cancer increased in every decade, and by 1993 it was 3.2 times as high as it was in 1900. Cardiovascular diseases, on the other hand, had a death rate in 1993 that was only 6 percent higher than it was in 1900. Violent deaths were 33 percent lower in 1993 than in 1900, and infectious diseases were 87 percent lower in 1993 than in 1900. Thus, cancer was the only leading cause of death to increase significantly during the century.

Violent deaths were relatively constant from 1900 through 1940, growing from a level of 83.7 in 1900 to 93.9 in 1940, with peaks near 104 in 1910 and 1930. Violent deaths fell after 1940, with only a small increase between 1960 and 1970 interrupting a steady decline from 1930 through 1993. But the pattern for the three components of violent deaths (accidents, suicide, and homicide) each varied in a different way. As shown in Figure 2-11, accidents slowly declined, suicide remained nearly constant, and homicide increased sharply.

Figure 2-7 shows results for the four groups as a percentage of total deaths.

Figure 2-6. Death Rates per 100,000 for Selected Causes

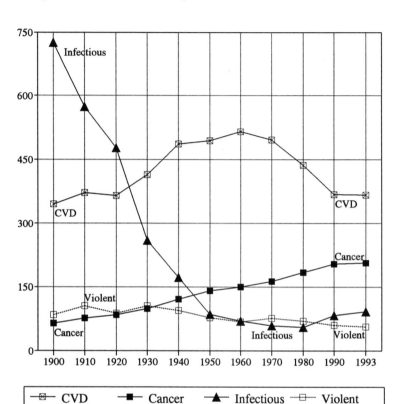

Year	CVD	Cancer	Infectious	Violent
1900	345.2	64.0	726.0	83.7
1910	371.9	76.2	572.6	104.1
1920	364.9	83.4	477.1	87.0
1930	414.4	97.4	259.1	104.3
1940	485.7	120.3	171.8	93.9
1950	494.4	139.8	84.6	77.3
1960	515.1	149.2	69.5	67.6
1970	496.0	162.8	58.2	76.3
1980	436.4	183.9	54.1	69.3
1990	368.3	203.2	82.1	59.4
1993	366.3	205.8	91.0	56.4

Figure 2-7 shows the percentage of total deaths accounted for by groups of causes that produced the most deaths from 1900 through 1993. Death rates rather than percentage of total deaths for these groups are shown in Figure 2-6. The groups are cardiovascular diseases (CVD), infectious diseases, cancer, and violent deaths. The exact percentages are shown numerically under the graph. Cardiovascular diseases include heart disease, stroke, and other cardiovascular diseases. Infectious diseases include pneumonia/flu, tuberculosis, chronic obstructive pulmonary diseases (COPD), and the other infectious diseases identified in Tables 2-1, 2-2, and 2-3. The "other" category encompasses nearly every infectious disease known to the general public, including HIV/AIDS. The violent group includes accidents of all types, suicide, and homicide.

Infectious diseases accounted for 42.2 percent of all deaths in 1900, more than twice the percentage for cardiovascular diseases. But while the death rate fell sharply after 1900 for infectious diseases (Figure 2-6), the percentage of total deaths fell rather slowly after 1900. This is because the overall death rate in the United States fell rapidly after 1900 (Figure 2-1). That means that as the death rate for infectious diseases fell in concert with the overall death rate, the percentage of deaths caused by infectious diseases fell much more slowly. This is one reason it is necessary to look at causes of death in terms of percentage of total deaths as well as in terms of absolute death rates to understand how the causes of death varied during the century.

Similarly, although cardiovascular diseases passed infectious diseases in the early 1920s in terms of percentage of total deaths, just as they had in terms of absolute death rates (Figure 2-6), what happened after the 1920s was substantially different. In terms of absolute death rates, cardiovascular diseases rose to a peak in 1960, but never got close to the peak reached by infectious diseases in 1900. That gives the impression that infectious diseases had the highest peak of all the causes of death in the century. But in terms of percentage of total deaths, in 1960 cardiovascular diseases soared far above the 42.2 percent peak exhibited by infectious diseases in 1900. Cardiovascular diseases accounted for 54.0 percent of all deaths in 1960, a level that was 28 percent above the peak of infectious diseases in 1900. In fact, cardiovascular diseases were above the peak level of infectious diseases constantly from 1940 through 1990. Cardiovascular diseases easily rank as the worst killer in the United States in the century.

From 1900 through 1993, cardiovascular diseases increased by 107 percent in percent of total deaths compared to only 6 percent in absolute death rate (Figure 2-6). Cancer increased 6.3 times in percent of total deaths compared to only 3.2 times in absolute death rate. Violent deaths increased by 31 percent in percent of total deaths compared to a 33 percent decline in absolute death rate. These differences are due to the decline of infectious diseases, which decreased 76 percent in percent of total deaths and 87 percent in absolute death rate.

Figure 2-7. Percent of Total Deaths for Selected Causes

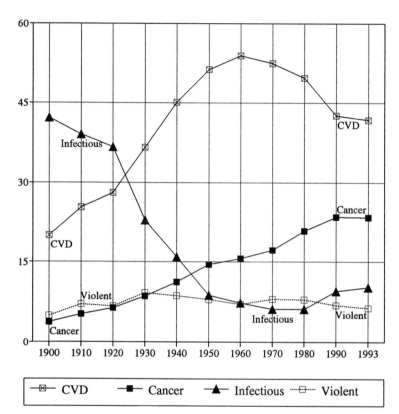

Year	CVD	Cancer	Infectious	Violent
1900	20.1%	3.7%	42.2%	4.9%
1910	25.3%	5.2%	39.0%	7.1%
1920	28.1%	6.4%	36.7%	6.7%
1930	36.6%	8.6%	22.9%	9.2%
1940	45.1%	11.2%	16.0%	8.7%
1950	51.3%	14.5%	8.8%	8.0%
1960	54.0%	15.6%	7.3%	7.1%
1970	52.5%	17.2%	6.2%	8.1%
1980	49.7%	20.9%	6.2%	7.9%
1990	42.6%	23.5%	9.5%	6.9%
1993	41.7%	23.4%	10.3%	6.4%

Figure 2-8 shows death rates for the four individual causes that were the leading causes of death in the second half of the century. The four causes are heart disease, cancer, stroke, and accidents. As shown in Table 2-2. these causes remained in the same rank order from 1950 through 1990, with accidents slipping to fifth place in 1993 while heart disease, cancer, and stroke remained in first, second, and third place respectively. The purpose of Figure 2-8 is to show how these causes varied over the full century even though they had much different rankings in the top ten lists earlier in the century. This permits a fuller understanding of the history of the individual causes of death that are the primary killers today.

Heart disease had the highest rate among the four causes in 1900 and was fifth on the top ten list (Table 2-1). Stoke was just behind heart disease among the four causes and was also just behind in fifth place on the overall list. Accidents were eighth on the overall list, just ahead of cancer in ninth place.

Heart disease rose slowly through 1920, but it became the leading cause of death from 1910 through 1917 before being replaced by pneumonia/flu during the global flu epidemic that peaked in 1918 and lasted through 1920. Heart disease reclaimed first place in 1921, and it has been the leading killer in the United States ever since. As shown in many of the preceding figures, heart disease peaked in the early 1960s and has been declining since.

The death rate for stroke fell slowly from 1900 through 1940, then moved up slowly from 1940 through 1960. The death rate for stroke peaked in the early 1960s concurrent with the peak for heart disease. The rate fell steadily after 1960 and reached a low point for the century in 1990, before turning up slightly in 1993. However, the age-adjusted rate has continued to fall (Part III).

Accidents have generally fallen during the century. The death rate due to accidents in 1940 was almost identical to that of 1900. But accidents other than motor vehicle accidents declined steadily after 1910, while motor vehicle accidents began a sharp increase. However, motor vehicle accidents declined from 1930 through 1960, jumped up to a peak for the century in 1970 (Figure 2-11), and then declined again. The net result was a steady decline in the death rate due to accidents of all kinds from 1930 through 1993, except for a small rise in 1970. The United States is a much safer place to work and play now than it was in 1900 in spite of the advent of the car and other motor vehicles.

The death rate for cancer has increased constantly throughout the century. It was at its peak level in 1993, and it is still increasing. However, as shown in detail in Part IV, the story of cancer would be completely different if people had stopped smoking early in the century. All of the increase in cancer deaths in the latter part of the century is due to increases in lung cancer for both men and women. This is one cause of death that is due almost entirely to lifestyle choices, and unfortunately the deadly choice for many persons is to smoke.

Figure 2-8. Death Rates per 100,000 for Top Causes Since 1950

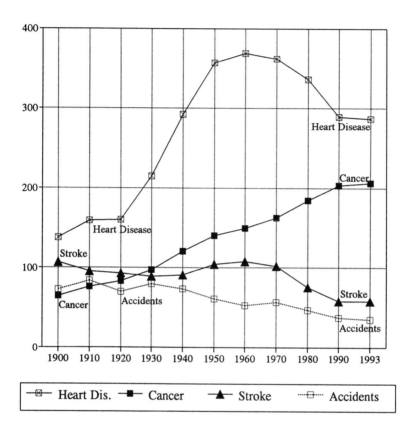

Year	Heart Disease	Cancer	Stroke	Accidents
1900	137.4	64.0	106.9	72.3
1910	158.9	76.2	95.8	84.2
1920	159.6	83.4	93.0	70.0
1930	214.2	97.4	89.0	79.8
1940	292.5	120.3	90.9	73.2
1950	356.8	139.8	104.0	60.6
1960	369.0	149.2	108.0	52.3
1970	362.0	162.8	101.9	56.4
1980	336.0	183.9	75.1	46.7
1990	289.5	203.2	57.9	37.0
1993	286.9	205.8	58.1	34.4

Figure 2-9 shows the percentage of total deaths accounted for by the four individual causes that were the leading causes of death in the second half of the century. The exact percentages are shown numerically in the table under the graph. The four causes are heart disease, cancer, stroke, and accidents. Death rates rather than percentage of total deaths for these four causes are shown in Figure 2-8.

As shown in Table 2-2, these causes remained in the same rank order from 1950 through 1990, with accidents slipping to fifth place in 1993 while heart disease, cancer, and stroke remained in first, second, and third place respectively. The purpose of Figure 2-9 is to show how the percentages of total deaths for these causes varied over the full century even though they had much different rankings in the top ten lists earlier in the century. This permits a fuller understanding of the history of the individual causes of death that are the primary killers today.

There are substantial differences between changes in percentage of total deaths and changes in the absolute death rate. This is because the overall death rate in the United States fell sharply between 1900 and 1993 (Figure 2-1). For example, heart disease increased by a factor of 2.1 between 1900 and 1993 in terms of absolute death rate (Figure 2-8). However, in terms of percentage of total deaths, it increased by a factor of 4.1. This means heart disease was a much more significant killer in 1993 compared to 1900 than the death rate comparison would suggest. This is one reason it is necessary to look at causes of death in terms of percentage of total deaths as well as in terms of absolute death rates to understand how the causes of death varied during the century.

Similarly, stroke declined by 46 percent in death rate between 1900 and 1993. However, in terms of percentage of total deaths, stroke did not decrease at all but actually increased by 6 percent. With many other causes of death sharply reduced in 1993 (primarily infectious diseases), the lower death rate for strokes in 1993 compared to 1900 actually accounts for a higher percentage of total deaths than did the much higher rate in 1900.

For cancer, the absolute death rate increased by a factor of 3.2 from 1900 through 1993. But in terms of percentage of total deaths, the increase was by a factor of 6.3 (23.4 percent compared to 3.7 percent). Going from accounting for about 1 death in 27 in 1900 to about 1 death in 4 in 1993 is one reason cancer evokes an increased sense of dread now compared to earlier in the century.

For accidents, the absolute death rate fell by 52 percent between 1900 and 1993. But in terms of percentage of total deaths, the decrease over the same period was only 7 percent. The absolute rate in 1900 was the third highest in the century, but, in terms of percentage of total deaths, 1900 had the lowest level in the century until 1993 posted a mark just under the 1900 percentage. Determining whether 1900 was a high or low point depends on the method of measurement.

Figure 2-9. Percent of Total Deaths for Top Causes Since 1950

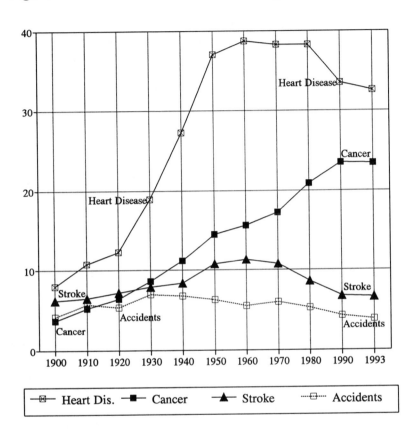

Year	Heart Disease	Cancer	Stroke	Accidents
1900	8.0%	3.7%	6.2%	4.2%
1910	10.8%	5.2%	6.5%	5.7%
1920	12.3%	6.4%	7.2%	5.4%
1930	18.9%	8.6%	7.9%	7.0%
1940	27.2%	11.2%	8.4%	6.8%
1950	37.0%	14.5%	10.8%	6.3%
1960	38.7%	15.6%	11.3%	5.5%
1970	38.3%	17.2%	10.8%	6.0%
1980	38.3%	20.9%	8.6%	5.3%
1990	33.5%	23.5%	6.8%	4.3%
1993	32.6%	23.4%	6.6%	3.9%

Figure 2-10 shows the variation in death rates from 1900 through 1993 for the key diseases included in the overall term "infectious diseases." The key diseases are pneumonia/flu, tuberculosis, and COPD/respiratory. COPD (chronic obstructive pulmonary diseases) was the term adapted by the International Classification of Diseases in 1975 to encompass several respiratory diseases (primarily bronchitis, emphysema, and asthma) that had previously been listed separately or in an "all other" category. Thus, the heading "COPD/Respiratory" is meant to include these various diseases from 1900 through 1993. The term "other" in Figure 2-10 includes all infectious diseases other than pneumonia/flu, tuberculosis, and COPD/respiratory. This means it is more inclusive than the term "other infectious" in Tables 2-1, 2-2, and 2-3, but it includes every disease listed in the other infectious category in those tables. The exact data for the four categories are shown numerically in the table under the graph.

Because of the many individual diseases it includes, the other category had the highest death rate among the four categories in Figure 2-10 in 1900 and 1910. The death rate for pneumonia/flu was just ahead of the rate for tuberculosis in 1900 and 1910, but tuberculosis actually had a higher rate than pneumonia/flu a total of six times in the ten years from 1900 through 1909. Thus, tuberculosis was the leading individual cause of death among all infectious diseases before 1910 (Table 2-1). Tuberculosis also was the leading individual cause of death among infectious diseases from 1911 through 1914. It was overtaken by pneumonia/flu in 1915, and pneumonia/flu remained the leading cause of death among infectious diseases until replaced by COPD in 1980.

The death rates for all infectious diseases fell sharply in the United States after 1900, and only the global flu epidemic of 1918 kept them from falling even more rapidly in the first two decades. The advent of antibiotic drugs started with some sulfa drugs in the 1930s, but antibiotics did not come into wide use until the 1940s, with World War II being a main catalyst in their use in the general population. But the death rates for infectious disease in the United States had already fallen dramatically before antibiotics due to improvements in public health and nutrition. This was not true in many other countries of the world (and still is not the case in most third-world countries).

The combination of good public health and antibiotics drove infectious diseases to a low point for the century in 1980. But the combination of an aging population (pneumonia/flu and COPD take their highest tolls among the elderly), infectious diseases that are drug-resistant, and a growing immigrant population from the third world led to an increase in the death rate from infectious diseases between 1980 and 1993. The fact that pneumonia/flu and COPD are still at the top means the main causative factor is the aging of the population. Even a deadly new disease like HIV/AIDS had a death rate of only 13.8 in 1993 (Table 2-3). But the new upturn does show infectious diseases will be with us indefinitely.

Figure 2-10. Death Rates per 100,000 for Infectious Causes

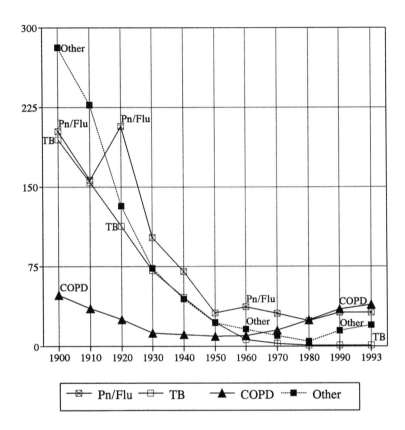

Year	Pneumonia/Flu	Tuberculosis	COPD/Respiratory	Other
1900	202.2	194.4	48.3	281.1
1910	155.9	153.8	35.6	227.3
1920	207.3	113.1	24.9	131.8
1930	102.5	71.1	12.3	73.2
1940	70.3	45.9	11.0	44.6
1950	31.3	22.5	9.0	21.8
1960	37.3	6.1	9.9	16.2
1970	30.9	2.6	15.2	9.5
1980	24.1	0.9	24.7	4.4
1990	32.0	0.7	34.9	14.5
1993	31.7	0.6	39.2	19.5

Figure 2-11 shows the variation in death rates from 1900 through 1993 for the key causes included in the overall term "violent causes" (Figure 2-6). These causes are motor vehicle and other accidents, suicide, and homicide. The exact rates are shown numerically in the table under the graph. Deaths from violent causes are due to circumstances outside the body rather than a disease process. This is why accidents and homicide are among the major causes of death before the age of 25 (Part V). There are relatively few disease processes that cause deaths in persons younger than 25.

Because motor vehicle accidents were not recorded separately in 1900, the table under the graph does not have a value for motor vehicle accidents for 1900. Instead the "(Vehicle)" heading shows the column is for motor vehicle accidents. The second column is for all other accidents. There were few motor vehicles on the road in 1910, and thus the death rate for such accidents was very low. The rate accelerated with the number of cars and trucks being produced, and by 1930 the death rate due to motor vehicle accidents was well above those for suicide and homicide. But 1930 marked a peak in deaths due to motor vehicle accidents. They fell from 1930 through 1960, rose again in 1970, and then declined steadily after 1970. By 1993 the rate was more than 40 percent below the nearly twin peaks of 1930 and 1970, in spite of the much higher number of cars and trucks on the road. This result is a credit to the excellent roads in the United States, much safer cars and trucks, and nearly universal driving training.

The results for all other accidents also reflects positively on the working conditions and general education about accident prevention in the United States. The death rate for all other accidents fell by 78 percent from 1910 through 1990 before increasing slightly between 1990 and 1993. The death rate due to accidents of all kinds decreased by 52 percent from 1900 through 1993 in spite of the growth of the driving population in the country. The United States is a much safer place to work and play today than at any time in the century.

The death rate for suicide varied from a low of 10.2 in 1900 and 1920 to a high of 15.6 in 1930 (probably a reflection of the stock market crash in 1929 and the beginning of the great depression of the 1930s). The range after 1950 was narrower, with a high of 12.4 in 1990 and a low of 10.6 in 1960. There is no evidence to support the supposition that the complicated world of today leads to more suicides. The fact that the average rate since 1950 is 11.6 compared to an average of 13.1 before 1950 leads to the opposite conclusion.

The death rate for homicide increased sharply after 1900, reaching a peak of 10.7 in 1980. This was nine times higher than in 1900. The rate declined by seven percent between 1980 and 1993. The present notoriety of homicide is primarily due to the 128 percent increase between 1960 and 1980. But the 1960 level was 47 percent below the previous peak in 1930, and the 1993 level was only 11 percent above the 1930 mark. The days of sharp increases may be over.

Figure 2-11. Death Rates per 100,000 for Violent Causes

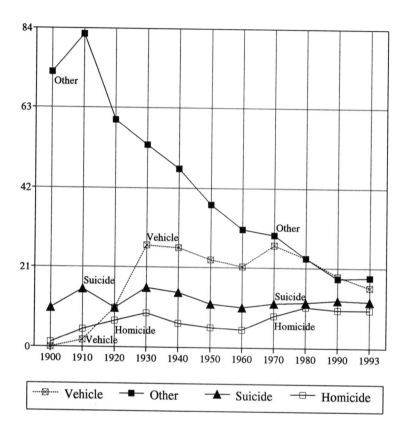

Year	Motor Vehicle/Other Accidents		Suicide	Homicide
1900	(Vehicle)	72.3	10.2	1.2
1910	1.8	82.4	15.3	4.6
1920	10.3	59.7	10.2	6.8
1930	26.7	53.1	15.6	8.9
1940	26.2	47.0	14.4	6.3
1950	23.1	37.5	11.4	5.3
1960	21.3	31.0	10.6	4.7
1970	26.9	29.5	11.6	8.3
1980	23.5	23.3	11.9	10.7
1990	18.8	18.2	12.4	10.0
1993	15.9	18.5	12.1	9.9

Figure 2-12 shows the variation from 1900 through 1993 of the percentage of total deaths from combined groups of causes that produce the majority of deaths in the United States (and in the world). The two combinations are cardiovascular diseases and cancer (CVD/Cancer), and infectious diseases and violent causes (Infectious/Violent). The percentage of total deaths and death rates for each combination are shown numerically in the table under the graph, but only the percentage is shown in the graph. The last column in the table under the graph shows the ratio of CVD/Cancer to infectious disease and violent causes.

The two combinations represent two different aspects of the causes of death. CVD and cancer are primarily chronic diseases that develop in the body over a long period of time. They basically represent decay of the systems in the body, although harmful substances introduced into the body by such actions as smoking and the abuse of drugs and alcohol can contribute substantially to the decay of systems in the body. Deaths due to infectious diseases and violent causes primarily represent attacks on the body from outside agents. The two combinations roughly represent deaths due to external and internal causes.

The percentage of total deaths due to infectious disease and violent causes in 1900 was nearly twice as high as the percentage for CVD/Cancer. This is shown by the 0.51 value for the ratio of the two combinations. As deaths due to CVD/Cancer increased while those due to infectious disease and violent causes decreased, the ratio climbed to 1.67 in 1930. This means the percentage of total deaths for CVD/Cancer was 67 percent higher than that for infectious disease and violent causes. The ratio peaked at 4.81 in 1960. As deaths due to CVD/Cancer decreased after 1960, the ratio gradually fell to 3.88 in 1993. This was a decline of 19 percent from the peak in 1960.

Intervention against deaths due to external causes was quite successful between 1900 and 1980. However, the percentage of total deaths due to infectious disease and violent causes rose by 20 percent between 1980 and 1993. As discussed in the text accompanying Figure 2-10, most of the increase was due to the aging of the population (elderly people are more vulnerable to attacks by infectious diseases). But the increase is a warning that vigilance is needed to keep the percentage of total deaths due to such causes from steadily increasing. The percentage of total deaths due to external causes has stayed below 20 percent since 1950, but the level in 1993 was exactly the same as in 1950 (16.8 percent), and thus marks the highest level in over 40 years.

The percentage of total deaths due to CVD/Cancer increased steadily from 1900 to 1980. The 1980 level of 70.6 percent was nearly three times as high as that of 1900. Much of this is due to the aging of the population, but the 8 percent decline between 1980 and 1993 shows that intervention can be made successfully against internal causes. Parts III and IV show cardiovascular diseases and cancer variations in detail to clarify the kind of intervention needed.

Figure 2-12. Percent of Deaths from Combined Selected Causes

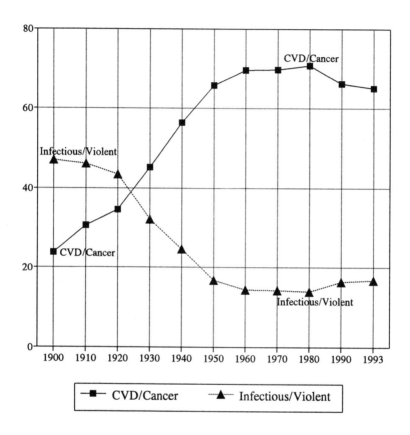

Year	CVD/Cancer Rate and %		Infectious/Violent		Ratio
1900	409.2	23.8%	809.7	47.1%	0.51
1910	448.1	30.5%	676.7	46.1%	0.66
1920	448.3	34.5%	564.1	43.4%	0.91
1930	511.8	45.2%	363.4	32.1%	1.67
1940	606.0	56.3%	265.7	24.7%	2.39
1950	634.2	65.8%	161.9	16.8%	4.10
1960	664.3	69.6%	137.1	14.4%	4.81
1970	658.8	69.7%	134.5	14.2%	4.61
1980	620.3	70.6%	123.4	14.0%	4.63
1990	571.5	66.2%	141.5	16.4%	4.04
1993	572.1	65.1%	147.4	16.8%	3.88

Part III
Cardiovascular
Diseases

Cardiovascular Diseases in Depth

Figure 3-1 shows the variation in death rates per 100,000 from 1900 through 1993 for the three main components of cardiovascular diseases. The three components are heart disease, stroke, and other cardiovascular diseases. The exact rates are shown numerically in the table under the graph.

The cardiovascular system consists essentially of the heart and the blood vessels that carry blood throughout the body. The major problems result from narrowing of the blood vessels over time and eventual blockage of an artery in the heart or the brain (and other organs). The result of a blockage in the heart is a heart attack, and the result of a blockage in the brain is a stroke. Blood vessels can also rupture. If one ruptures in the brain it also causes a stoke (and often sudden death), while ruptures elsewhere can cause catastrophic loss of blood. The heart is also subject to disease processes that impair its ability to pump blood efficiently. Congestive heart failure is one result of these processes. Other system failures due to related disease processes, as well as problems due to high blood pressure, are combined in the term "other" cardiovascular diseases.

Between 1900 and 1920, the death rates for heart disease, stroke, and other cardiovascular diseases were relatively close. After 1920 the death rate for heart disease began to increase sharply, while stoke and other cardiovascular diseases remained close together through 1940. Between 1940 and 1950 the death rate for other cardiovascular diseases fell by 67 percent. A substantial part of this decline was the redefinition of the causes of death in the Sixth Revision of the International Causes of Death in 1949. This change increased death rates for heart disease and stroke, while other cardiovascular diseases accounted for only about 6 percent of total deaths due to cardiovascular diseases after 1950.

The death rate for stoke was relatively constant from 1900 through 1970, with a small increase from 1950 through 1970 due primarily to the redefinition of 1949. The stroke death rate fell by 43 percent between 1970 and 1993 as part of the sharp reduction in death rates for heart disease and stroke that took place after the 1960s. The death rate for heart disease fell by 22 percent from 1960 through 1993. These reductions were primarily due to improvements in medical technology and the response of many persons in the population to the educational material provided by many sources about the changes in lifestyle needed to reduce cardiovascular diseases. The decline in death rates was even more dramatic on an age-adjusted basis as shown in Figure 3-2.

Figure 3-1. Cardiovascular Death Rates per 100,000

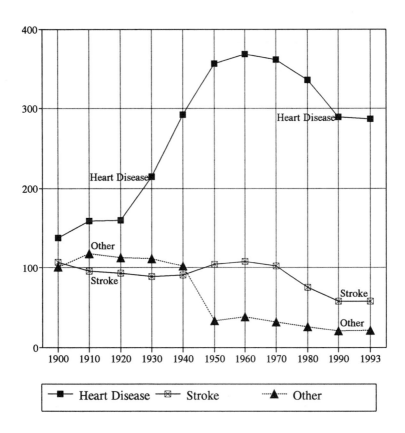

Year	Heart Disease	Stroke	Other
1900	137.4	106.9	100.9
1910	158.9	95.8	117.2
1920	159.6	93.0	112.3
1930	214.2	89.0	111.2
1940	292.5	90.9	102.3
1950	356.8	104.0	33.6
1960	369.0	108.0	38.1
1970	362.0	101.9	32.1
1980	336.0	75.1	25.3
1990	289.5	57.9	20.9
1993	286.9	58.1	21.3

Figure 3-2 shows the variation from 1940 through 1990 of the age-adjusted death rates per 100,000 for three components of cardiovascular diseases (CVD). In this case, the three components (coronary heart disease, stroke, and other cardiovascular diseases) are based on definitions used by the American Heart Association. These definitions are not necessarily the same as those used in the rest of the book, and thus the exact values shown numerically under the graph can not be compared directly to the values used in the rest of the book. But the main purpose of Figure 3-2 is to show variations in the death rates, and thus the key data in Figure 3-2 are the percentage declines from 1940 through 1990 that are also shown in the table under the graph. The age-adjusted reference year for Figure 3-2 is 1940 (the discussion in the text accompanying Figure 2-1 explains the use of reference years in presenting data on an age-adjusted basis). This is why Figure 3-2 begins at 1940.

The term "heart disease" in Figure 3-2 is coronary heart disease only. This is the disease process that is commonly known as a "heart attack." It accounts for about two-thirds of all deaths due to heart disease. From its peak of 235.4 in 1960, the age-adjusted death rate for coronary heart disease fell by 52 percent by 1990. The overall decline from 1940 through 1990 was 45.7 percent as shown in the table under the graph. These dramatic declines give greater emphasis to the results that can be obtained from changing lifestyles as described in Part V. The decline of coronary heart disease (and total heart disease) in the last part of the Twentieth Century is one of the great success stories in disease prevention.

Age-adjusted death rates for stroke fell by 72.6 percent from 1940 through 1990, with a 59 percent decline just between 1970 and 1990. This is an even more dramatic decline in percentage terms than that of coronary heart disease, but coronary heart disease accounts for more that three times as many deaths as stroke (Figure 2-3), and thus declines in coronary heart disease save more lives. But the 72.6 percent decline in stroke is another success story in combining changes in lifestyle with improvements in medical technology. The key medical improvement in this case was the development of improved drugs to reduce high blood pressure. But the drugs would be of little help if efforts had not been made to get people to have their blood pressure checked.

The percentage drop (88.0 percent) in the age-adjusted death rate for other cardiovascular diseases was even greater than those for coronary heart disease and stroke. On a combined basis, the death rate for all three components was 401.9 in 1940. By 1990 the combined rate was 152.3, a decline of 62 percent. The age-adjusted death rates are continuing to decline, and the even better news is that the rate accounting for the most deaths (coronary heart disease) is decreasing the most rapidly. These data confirm that an increasingly older population does not have to mean an increasingly infirm population, if the proper steps are taken to prevent the onset of chronic diseases.

Figure 3-2. CVD Age-Adjusted Death Rates per 100,000

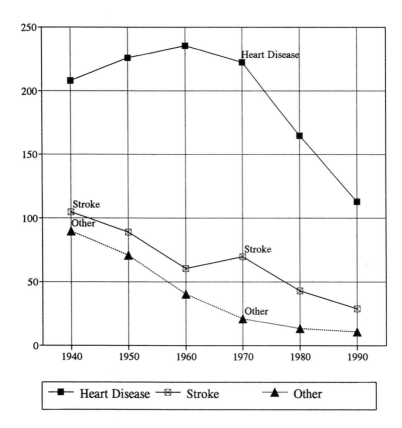

Year	Heart Disease	Stroke	Other
1940	207.6	104.6	89.7
1950	225.6	88.7	70.8
1960	235.4	60.4	40.3
1970	222.1	69.7	20.8
1980	164.6	42.6	13.3
1990	112.8	28.7	10.8

Declines from 1940 through 1990:

    H. Disease   45.7% (coronary heart disease only)

    Stroke   72.6%

    Other   88.0%

Note: Age-adjusted reference year is 1940.

Figure 3-3 shows the variation from 1950 through 1992 of the death rates per 100,000 for heart disease for the total population and for males and females. The exact rates are shown numerically in the table under the graph. The table also shows the ratio of the rate for males to the rate for females, as well as the percentage declines from 1950 through 1992 for each of the three rates in the graph and the male-to-female ratio.

The overall rate shows a pattern similar to that seen in other figures in the book related to heart disease, i.e., a peak in 1960 and an appreciable decline afterwards. But the pattern of the changes in death rates for males and females are quite different from each other. The rate for males peaked in 1960 and fell sharply afterwards (the apparently smaller decline in the last years shown in the graph is a little misleading because the last two points are only two years apart due to the availability of complete data). The rate for females did not peak until 1980 and fell more slowly after its peak than did the rate for males. The result is that the death rates for males and females have grown steadily closer.

As shown by the ratio in the table under the graph, males had a death rate that was 47 percent higher than that of females in 1950 (ratio of 1.47). But by 1992, the difference was only 4 percent (ratio of 1.04). This means the present overall death rate for heart disease is nearly the same for males and females.

The percentage declines shown in the table under the graph outline clearly how the rates for males and females grew constantly closer together from 1950 through 1992. The rate for males declined by 32.4 percent from 1950 through 1992, while the rate for females declined by only 4.8 percent over the same period. This means the ratio between the two declined by 29.0 percent, bringing it very close to the 1.0 value that means identical rates for each group.

These results seem to conflict with prior discussions pointing out that women have an inherent advantage over men in protection from heart disease prior to menopause, and a lower death rate due to heart disease at all ages thereafter. But the data for deaths due to heart disease have the same flaw shared by all such data when used to measure the difference in death rates between males and females. As shown clearly in Part I, women have a greater life expectancy than men at all ages. This means that as the population ages, there will be more women than men in the total population. It also means that samples of the population based on gender will not have the same age distribution. A group of 100,000 men will have an average age lower than a group of 100,000 women. Thus, "raw" death rates that do not take this difference into account will not give a complete picture of differences in death rate due to gender.

The best way to get a clear picture of the differences due to gender is to use age-adjusted data. Figure 3-4 shows the results for such data using the same definitions for heart disease as used in Figure 3-3 (and in the rest of the book except for Figure 3-2).

Figure 3-3. Male/Female Heart Disease Death Rates per 100,000

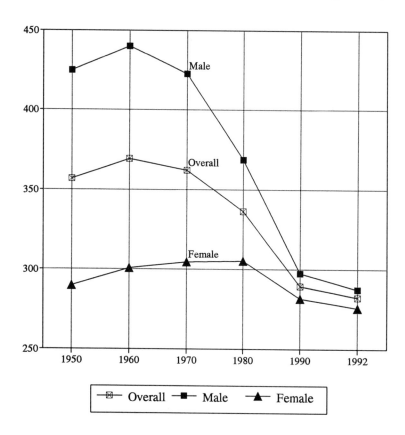

Year	Overall	Male	Female	Ratio
1950	356.8	424.7	289.7	1.47
1960	369.0	439.5	300.6	1.46
1970	362.0	422.5	304.5	1.39
1980	336.0	368.6	305.1	1.21
1990	289.5	297.6	281.8	1.06
1992	282.5	287.2	275.8	1.04

Declines from 1950 through 1992:

Overall	20.8%
Male	32.4%
Female	4.8%
Ratio	29.0%

Figure 3-4 shows the variation from 1960 through 1990 of age-adjusted death rates per 100,000 for heart disease for the total population and for males and females. The exact rates are shown numerically in the table under the graph. The table also shows the ratio of the rate for males to the rate for females, as well as the percentage declines from 1960 through 1990 for each of the three rates in the graph and the male-to-female ratio. The age-adjusted reference year for the data is 1940. The text accompanying Figure 2-1 explains the use of age-adjusted data and the significance of the reference year.

The results of Figure 3-4 are quite different than those of Figure 3-3 which showed the same variations using "raw" (not age-adjusted) data. Figure 3-4 shows that the decline in death rates due to heart disease are nearly identical for males and females on an age-adjusted basis. As shown in the table under the graph, the rate for males declined by 45.0 percent while the rate for females declined by 47.1 percent between 1960 and 1990. Figure 3-3 using raw data showed a large decline for males but a very small decline for females.

The ratio in the table under the graph shows that males had a rate 83 percent higher than that of females in 1960 (ratio of 1.83). The ratio changed very little by 1990 when males had a rate 90 percent higher than that for females (ratio of 1.90). The fact that the ratio actually increased means that the "decline" shown in the table is a negative 4.0 percent, i.e., an increase of 4.0 percent. But for all practical purposes the ratio was constant from 1960 through 1990. This means that the decline in the overall rate for the total population (46.9 percent) was nearly identical to that for males and females individually.

Figure 3-4 confirms that women have lower death rates than men for heart disease, and the decline in death rates since 1960 is much the same for each gender. Also, the 46.9 percent decline in age-adjusted death rates for the total population from 1960 through 1990 is very close to the 52.1 percent decline shown in Figure 3-2, even though Figure 3-2 used a different definition for "heart disease," as explained in the text accompanying Figure 3-2. The advantages of age-adjusted data in determining changes in death rates over time is very clear when comparing Figures 3-1 and 3-2 and Figures 3-3 and 3-4.

Another way to eliminate the problem of comparing groups that have different age distributions in their sample populations is to compare results for various age groups in each population. For example, if the death rates for a specific disease for all persons in a fixed age bracket in one population group are compared with persons in the same age bracket in another population group, then problems with different age distributions in the two population groups are eliminated. This technique is used in the rest of the figures in this part of the book, and it is also used in many of the figures and tables in Part IV and Part V. Figure 3-5 shows death rates from two components of heart disease for males in the 45-54 age bracket.

Figure 3-4. Male/Female Age-Adjusted Heart Disease Rates

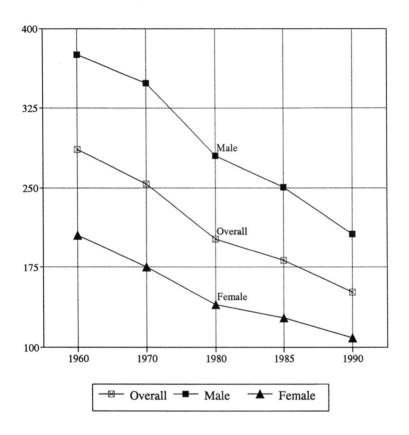

Year	Overall	Male	Female	Ratio
1960	286.2	375.5	205.7	1.83
1970	253.6	348.5	175.2	1.99
1980	202.0	280.4	140.3	2.00
1985	181.4	250.1	127.4	1.96
1990	152.0	206.7	108.9	1.90

Declines from 1960 through 1990:

Overall	46.9%
Male	45.0%
Female	47.1%
Ratio	-4.0% (Ratio increased by 4.0%)

Note: Age-adjusted reference year is 1940.

Figure 3-5 shows the variation from 1950 through 1992 of death rates per 100,000 for total heart disease, ischemic heart disease, and other heart disease for males in the 45-54 age bracket. The exact rates are shown numerically in the table under the graph. The table also shows the ratio of the rate for ischemic heart disease to the rate for other heart disease, as well as the percentage declines from 1950 through 1992 for each of the three rates in the graph and the ratio of ischemic heart disease and other heart disease.

Ischemic heart disease defines heart disease due to the blockage of an artery (or arteries) that supply the heart with blood. This is essentially what is meant by coronary heart disease or more commonly "heart attacks." Other heart disease includes all disease processes included in the term "heart disease" other than ischemic heart disease.

Figure 3-5 shows that death rates for total heart disease have been falling since 1950. Ischemic heart disease peaked in 1960, fell slightly by 1970, and then fell by 66 percent between 1970 and 1992. This drop brought the death rate for total heart disease down by 54 percent between 1970 and 1992. The drop was less for total heart disease because deaths due to other heart disease increased between 1970 and 1992.

The increase in other heart disease deaths was not due per se to an increase in other disease processes. In 1970 the ratio between ischemic heart disease and other heart disease was 8.80. This means that in 1970 other heart disease only accounted for 10 percent of all deaths due to heart disease. As deaths due to ischemic heart disease plummeted after 1970, deaths due to other causes became a more significant factor. In 1970 a man in the 45-54 age bracket died of a heart attack before other factors could cause problems. By 1992 the heart attack death rate in this bracket had fallen so far that the effect of other factors could be felt. In 1992 the ratio of ischemic heart disease to other heart disease was 1.95, and other heart disease was causing about one-third of all deaths due to heart disease for men in the 45-54 bracket.

The decline in death rates for total heart disease was 60.6 percent from 1950 through 1992. For the same period, the rate for ischemic heart disease fell by 63.7 percent, and the rate for other heart disease by 52.8 percent. The ratio of the ischemic heart disease rate to the rate for other heart disease declined by 23.1 percent. No matter how the decline was measured, deaths due to heart disease fell sharply for men in the 45-54 age bracket in the second half of the Twentieth Century.

These declines were due primarily to changes in lifestyle advocated by health groups after the connection between various behaviors and heart disease death rates were established by many studies. Advances in the treatment of men suffering heart attacks also contributed to the decline in deaths. Figure 3-6 shows that the decline was not just a result of pushing the deaths off to a later date.

Figure 3-5. Male Heart Disease Death Rates/100,000 (Age 45-54)

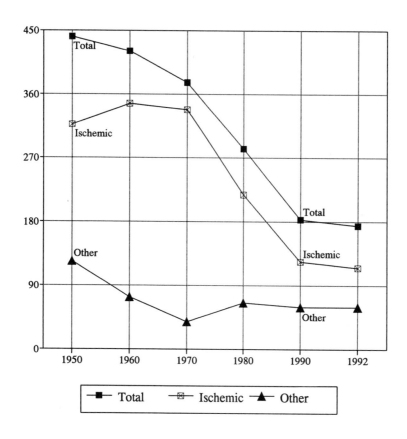

Year	Total	Ischemic	Other	Ratio
1950	441.2	316.6	124.6	2.54
1960	420.4	347.2	73.2	4.74
1970	376.4	338.0	38.4	8.80
1980	282.6	217.3	65.3	3.33
1990	183.0	123.8	59.2	2.09
1992	173.7	114.9	58.8	1.95

Declines from 1950 through 1992:

Total	60.6%
Ischemic	63.7%
Other	52.8%
Ratio	23.1%

Figure 3-6 shows the variation from 1950 through 1992 of death rates per 100,000 for total heart disease, ischemic heart disease, and other heart disease for males in the 55-64 age bracket. The exact rates are shown numerically in the table under the graph. The table also shows the ratio of the rate for ischemic heart disease to the rate for other heart disease, as well as the percentage declines from 1950 through 1992 for each of the three rates in the graph and the ratio of ischemic heart disease and other heart disease.

Ischemic heart disease defines heart disease due to the blockage of an artery (or arteries) that supply the heart with blood. This is essentially what is meant by coronary heart disease or more commonly "heart attacks." Other heart disease includes all disease processes included in the term "heart disease" other than ischemic heart disease.

Figure 3-6 shows that death rates in the 55-64 age bracket for males for total heart disease fell steadily after 1950. Ischemic heart disease peaked in 1970, and then fell by 62 percent between 1970 and 1992. This drop brought the death rate for total heart disease down by 49 percent between 1970 and 1992. The drop was less for total heart disease because deaths due to other heart disease increased between 1970 and 1992.

The increase in other heart disease deaths was not due per se to an increase in other disease processes. In 1970 the ratio between ischemic heart disease and other heart disease was 11.0. This means that in 1970 other heart disease only accounted for 8 percent of all deaths due to heart disease. As deaths due to ischemic heart disease plummeted after 1970, deaths due to other causes became a more significant factor. In 1970 a man in the 55-64 age bracket died of a heart attack before other factors could cause problems. By 1992 the heart attack death rate in this age bracket had fallen so far that the effect of other factors could be felt. In 1992 the ratio of ischemic heart disease to other heart disease was 2.17, and other heart disease was causing about one-third of all deaths due to heart disease for men in the 55-64 bracket.

The decline in death rates for total heart disease was 54.2 percent from 1950 through 1992. For the same period, the rate for ischemic heart disease fell by 56.5 percent, and the rate for other heart disease by 48.4 percent. The ratio of the ischemic heart disease rate to the rate for other heart disease declined by 15.7 percent. These declines were due primarily to changes in lifestyle advocated by health groups after the connection between various behaviors and heart disease death rates were established by many studies. Advances in the treatment of men suffering heart attacks also contributed to the decline in deaths.

The declines of Figure 3-6 are quite similar to those of Figure 3-5, even though the absolute values are much higher in Figure 3-6 due to the higher age bracket. The similar pattern of decline in both of age brackets means the onset of high heart disease death rates was being pushed well past age 65.

Figure 3-6. Male Heart Disease Death Rates/100,000 (Age 55-64)

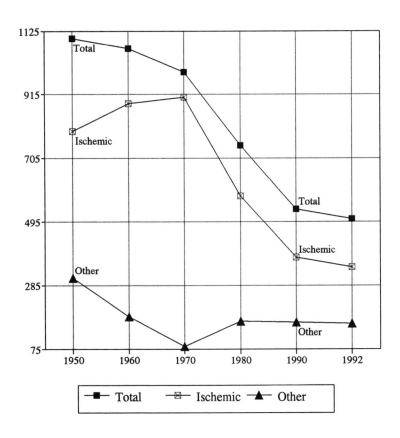

Year	Total	Ischemic	Other	Ratio
1950	1100.5	792.9	307.6	2.58
1960	1066.9	885.2	181.7	4.87
1970	987.2	904.6	82.6	11.0
1980	746.8	581.1	165.7	3.51
1990	537.3	375.4	161.9	2.32
1992	503.9	345.1	158.8	2.17

Declines from 1950 through 1992:

Total	54.2%
Ischemic	56.5%
Other	48.4%
Ratio	15.7%

Figure 3-7 shows the variation from 1950 through 1992 of death rates per 100,000 for total heart disease, ischemic heart disease, and other heart disease for females in the 45-54 age bracket. The exact rates are shown numerically in the table under the graph. The table also shows the ratio of the rate for ischemic heart disease to the rate for other heart disease, as well as the percentage declines from 1950 through 1992 for each of the three rates in the graph and the ratio of ischemic heart disease and other heart disease.

Ischemic heart disease defines heart disease due to the blockage of an artery (or arteries) that supply the heart with blood. This is essentially what is meant by coronary heart disease or more commonly "heart attacks." Other heart disease includes all disease processes included in the term "heart disease" other than ischemic heart disease.

Figure 3-7 shows that death rates for females in the 45-54 age bracket for total heart disease fell sharply after 1950. The decline from 1950 through 1992 was 67.3 percent. Ischemic heart disease peaked in 1970, and then fell by 62 percent between 1970 and 1992. This drop brought the death rate for total heart disease down by 47 percent between 1970 and 1992. The rate for other heart disease fell by 75 percent between 1950 and 1970, and then changed very little from 1970 through 1992.

The absolute rate for total heart disease for females in the 45-54 age bracket was 60 percent below that of males in the same age bracket in 1950 (Figure 3-5). By 1992 the female rate was 67 percent below that for males. The rate for ischemic heart disease (heart attacks) for females was 76 percent below that for males in 1950 and 72 percent below in 1992. This is a result of the inherent advantage in protection from heart attacks that women have before menopause compared to men.

One result of this protection is that the ratio of ischemic heart disease to other heart disease is much lower for women than for men. Other heart disease had a higher rate in 1950, and after the rate for ischemic heart disease moved above that for other heart disease in 1960, the two were very close again by 1990. Other problems are more important for women because the rate of ischemic heart disease is so low. Other heart disease accounted for 57 percent of all deaths in 1950 and 46 percent in 1992 for women in the 45-54 age bracket.

The decline in death rates for total heart disease was 67.3 percent from 1950 through 1992. For the same period, the rate for ischemic heart disease fell by 58.4 percent, and the rate for other heart disease by 74.0 percent. The ratio of the ischemic heart disease rate to the rate for other heart disease declined by a negative 59.7 percent, meaning that it increased by 59.7 percent. Except for the difference in the ratio as discussed above, these declines are similar to those for men even though the absolute levels were much lower for women. Thus, the lifestyle changes helping men helped women as well.

Figure 3-7. Female Heart Disease D. Rates/100,000 (Age 45-54)

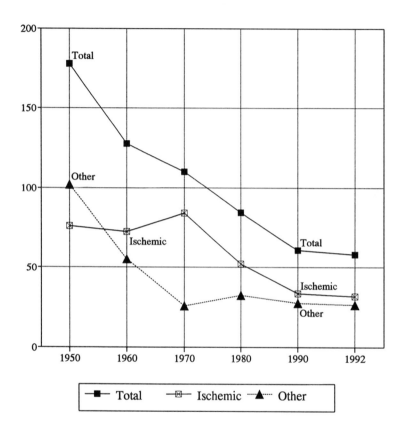

Year	Total	Ischemic	Other	Ratio
1950	177.8	76.0	101.8	0.75
1960	127.5	72.4	55.1	1.31
1970	109.9	84.0	25.9	3.24
1980	84.5	52.2	32.3	1.62
1990	61.0	33.6	27.4	1.23
1992	58.1	31.6	26.5	1.19

Declines from 1950 through 1992:

Total	67.3%
Ischemic	58.4%
Other	74.0%
Ratio	-59.7% (Ratio increased by 59.7%)

Figure 3-8 shows the variation from 1950 through 1992 of death rates per 100,000 for total heart disease, ischemic heart disease, and other heart disease for females in the 55-64 age bracket. The exact rates are shown numerically in the table under the graph. The table also shows the ratio of the rate for ischemic heart disease to the rate for other heart disease, as well as the percentage declines from 1950 through 1992 for each of the three rates in the graph and the ratio of ischemic heart disease and other heart disease.

Ischemic heart disease defines heart disease due to the blockage of an artery (or arteries) that supply the heart with blood. This is essentially what is meant by coronary heart disease or more commonly "heart attacks." Other heart disease includes all disease processes included in the term "heart disease" other than ischemic heart disease.

Figure 3-8 shows that death rates in the 55-64 age bracket for females for total heart disease fell steadily after 1950. Ischemic heart disease peaked in 1970, and then fell by 58 percent between 1970 and 1992. This drop brought the death rate for total heart disease down by 42 percent between 1970 and 1992. The drop was less for total heart disease because deaths due to other heart disease increased between 1970 and 1992.

From 1950 through 1992, the decline in death rates for total heart disease was 59.6 percent. For the same period, the rate for ischemic heart disease fell by 53.9 percent, and the rate for other heart disease by 66.3 percent. The ratio of the ischemic heart disease rate to the rate for other heart disease declined by a negative 36.7 percent, meaning that there was actually an increase of 36.7 percent.

The pattern of variation shown in Figure 3-8 is similar to that of Figure 3-6 for males in the 55-64 age bracket. This is different than the results for males and females in the 45-54 age bracket as shown by Figures 3-5 and 3-7. The difference is due to the fact that the development of heart disease is more similar in men and women after women pass the age of menopause, even though the absolute rates are still much lower in women. For example, the rate of total heart disease for women in the 55-64 age bracket was 59 percent lower than that of men in 1992 (in the 45-54 age bracket the difference was 67 percent). But the pattern of the variation of the disease over time becomes closer. The percentage of deaths caused by ischemic heart disease also becomes closer. For example, in women in the 55-64 age bracket, ischemic heart disease caused 62 percent of all deaths due to heart disease in 1992. For men in the same bracket the percentage was 68 percent. In the 45-54 age bracket the respective percentages were 54 percent for women and 66 percent for men.

The narrowing of the gap between men and women in terms of the total heart disease death rate is shown more clearly in Figure 3-9. This figure compares the rates for six different age brackets.

Figure 3-8. Female Heart Disease D. Rates/100,000 (Age 55-64)

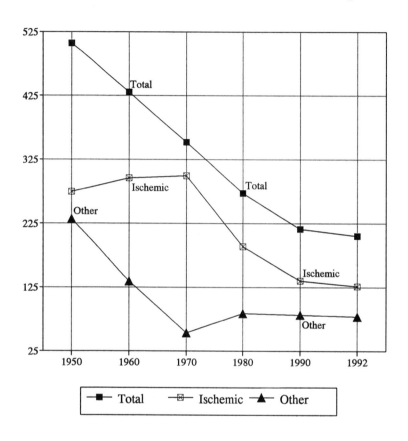

Year	Total	Ischemic	Other	Ratio
1950	507.0	275.0	232.0	1.19
1960	429.4	295.6	133.8	2.21
1970	351.6	299.1	52.5	5.70
1980	272.1	189.0	83.1	2.27
1990	215.7	135.4	80.3	1.69
1992	204.9	126.7	78.2	1.62

Declines from 1950 through 1992:

Total	59.6%	
Ischemic	53.9%	
Other	66.3%	
Ratio	-36.7%	(Ratio increased by 36.7%)

Figure 3-9 shows death rates per 100,000 for total heart disease for the overall population and for males and females in six age brackets. The brackets are 35-44, 45-54, 55-64, 65-74, 75-84, and 85 up. The exact rates are shown numerically in the table under the graph. The table also shows the ratio of the rate for male heart disease to the rate for female heart disease, as well as the ratio for all of the measures at age 85 up compared to the 35-44 age bracket.

At all ages the death rate for males is substantially higher than that for females, but the difference narrows in each successive age bracket (except for the change between the 35-44 bracket and the 45-54 bracket). This is shown by the ratio between males and females falling from 2.97 in the 35-44 bracket to 1.14 for the 85 up bracket. This means that the difference between males and females was only 14 percent in the 85 up bracket compared to 197 percent in the 35-44 bracket. Similarly, in the 35-44 bracket, the rate for males was 50 percent above the overall rate, while the rate for females was 49 percent below. But in the 85 up bracket, males were only 10 percent above the overall rate while females were only 4 percent below.

Regardless of gender, Figure 3-9 shows clearly how the death rate for total heart disease increases sharply with age. Because males have a much higher rate in the younger age brackets, the increase for males between the 35-44 bracket and the 85 up bracket is much less than that for females. This is shown by the ratios at the bottom of the table. The overall rate is 205 times higher in the 85 up bracket than in the 35-44 bracket. For males the rate in the 85 up bracket is 150 times as high as in the 35-44 bracket, while for females the rate in the 85 up bracket is 389 times as high as in the 35-44 bracket. The ratio between males and females in the 85 up bracket is only 0.38 of its value in the 35-44 bracket.

If there were an equal number of males and females in each age bracket, the overall death rate would be the average between the male and female rates. But the overall rate is always less than the average between the male and female rates. This fact, combined with the fact that the female rate is lower than the male rate in all brackets, means that there must more females in each age bracket. This is another measure of the fact that women live longer than men at all ages. It also means that more women die of heart disease than men, even though men have a higher rate per 100,000. For example, above the age of 65, about 20 percent more women than men die of heart disease, even though the rate for men is 23 percent higher than the rate for women. Heart disease is often thought of as a "man's disease," but the total number of women who die from heart disease is greater than that of men, and heart disease kills far more women than any other cause of death.

The second leading cause of death for both men and women is cancer, and in this case men hold the lead in both death rate and total deaths. Part IV provides a detailed look at death rates for cancer.

Figure 3-9. Male/Female Heart Disease D. Rates/100,000 by Age

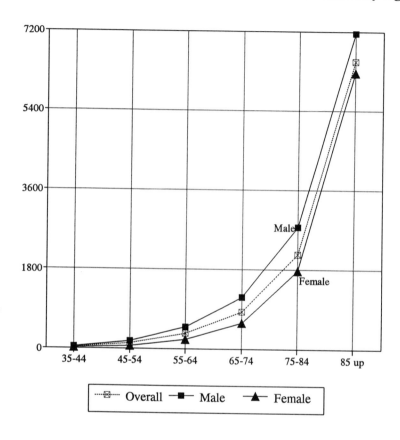

Age	Overall	Male	Female	Ratio
35-44	31.8	47.8	16.1	2.97
45-54	114.6	173.7	58.1	2.99
55-64	346.5	503.9	204.9	2.46
65-74	847.9	1178.8	587.8	2.01
75-84	2147.3	2754.0	1776.2	1.55
85 up	6513.5	7156.5	6263.1	1.14

Increase at 85 up compared to 35-44 (ratio):

Overall	205
Male	150
Female	389
Ratio	0.38

Part IV
Cancer

Cancer Death Rates in Depth

Figure 4-1 shows the variation in the cancer death rate per 100,000 from 1900 through 1993. The figure also shows a normalized death rate that assumes an equal percentage increase in the cancer death rate for each decade between 1900 and 1990. The exact rates are shown numerically in the table under the graph, together with the ratio of the actual rate to the normalized rate.

The use of the normalized rate makes it possible to see during which periods the cancer death rate increased more rapidly than the average for the century, and during which periods it increased less rapidly. For example, in 1910 the ratio between the actual rate and the normalized rate was 1.047. This means the actual rate grew 4.7 percent faster than the average rate between 1900 and 1910. The most rapid increase in the century came between 1930 and 1950. In 1930 the ratio was 1.035, meaning that the actual rate grew only 3.5 percent faster than the average rate from 1900 through 1930. But by 1940 the ratio was 1.125, and by 1950 it was 1.15. This means the actual rate grew 15 percent faster than the average rate from 1900 through 1950. The ratio declined in every decade after 1950, meaning the rate of increase after 1950 was less than the average for the century. This means that the steady growth of the cancer death rate from 1900 through 1993 was not due simply to the general aging of the population.

Determining the reasons for the steady growth of cancer during the century requires looking closely at the difference between cancer in males and females. Cancer is a group of diseases which behave differently in different sites in the body. The official term for cancer is malignant neoplasms. Neoplasms are new and abnormal formations of tissue which serve no useful function and which grow at the expense of the healthy organism in which they form. They are not usually life threatening unless they become malignant, i.e., they infiltrate the tissue in which they are formed and metastasize (spread via the bloodstream and the lymphatic system) to other parts of the body. Then they cause death by essentially diverting the nutrients of the body for their own use as they grow larger and larger while preventing the multiple organs in which they are now growing from performing their necessary functions.

Since the reproductive organs in males and females are different or perform different functions, the kind of cancers that arise and the effects they have on the body can be quite different. Thus, it is necessary to study the growth of cancer in different sites in males and females to learn how to prevent it.

Figure 4-1. Cancer Death Rates per 100,000

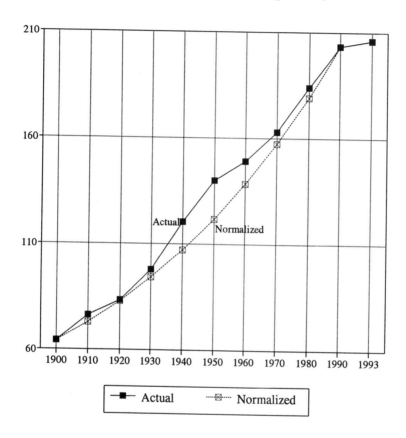

Year	Actual	Normalized	Ratio
1900	64.0	64.0	1.000
1910	76.2	72.8	1.047
1920	83.4	82.7	1.008
1930	97.4	94.1	1.035
1940	120.3	106.9	1.125
1950	139.8	121.6	1.150
1960	149.2	138.3	1.079
1970	162.8	157.2	1.036
1980	183.9	178.7	1.029
1990	203.2	203.2	1.000
1993	205.8	205.8	1.000

Figure 4-2 shows cancer death rates per 100,000 for the overall population and for males and females from 1940 through 1992. The exact rates are shown numerically in the table under the graph. The table also shows the ratio of the rate for males to the rate for females, as well as the increases from 1940 through 1992 of the three rates shown in the graph.

At the starting point of 1940, females had a higher cancer death rate than males. A dramatic decrease in uterine cancer death rates after 1940 (Figure 4-5) brought the female rate below the male rate by 1950, and it has stayed below ever since. The ratio of the male cancer rate to the female cancer rate peaked at 1.26 in 1970 (meaning the male rate was 26 percent higher than the female rate), and by 1992 the ratio was down to 1.17 or a difference of 17 percent.

The overall cancer rate increased by 69.8 percent from 1940 through 1992, while the male rate increased by 93.5 percent and the female rate increased by 48.9 percent. These results suggest that the cancer death rate is increasing alarmingly and no progress is being made against the disease. But as will be shown later in Part IV, death rates for nearly all forms of cancer are presently on the decline or growing very slowly. All of the increase in the cancer death rate for both males and females is due to lung cancer. Ironically, lung cancer is the one form of cancer that is most preventable. If no one smoked, the death rate for lung cancer would be so small that it would have no appreciable effect on overall cancer death rates. This is one clear case where people are literally killing themselves as a result of a lifestyle choice.

The increases in cancer death rates from 1940 through 1992 are much greater for males than for females. But if 1960 is taken as the reference point, the results are much different. From 1960 through 1992, the overall rate increased by 36.9 percent, the male rate by 35.9 percent, and the female rate by 38.0 percent. Thus, the rate of increase for the last three decades has been nearly the same for both males and females. This is shown also by the nearly identical ratios in 1960 and 1992. Thus, the conclusion can be made that recent rates of increase show very little difference by gender.

However, as noted before, raw death rate data as used in Figure 4-2 can be misleading when drawing conclusions about the different death rates for males and females. The average age distribution of females in the general population is higher than that of males. This is because, as shown in Part I, women live longer than men. Since cancer death rates increase with age (as do nearly all death rates due to disease), the results for women are overstated using raw data. This means it is necessary to use age-adjusted data to draw appropriate conclusions on the differences between males and females for a specific death rate comparison. Figure 4-3 uses age-adjusted data for the period after 1960 where it was concluded that the increases in cancer death rates were nearly equal for males and females. Figure 4-3 gives a quite different result.

Figure 4-2. Male/Female Cancer Death Rates per 100,000

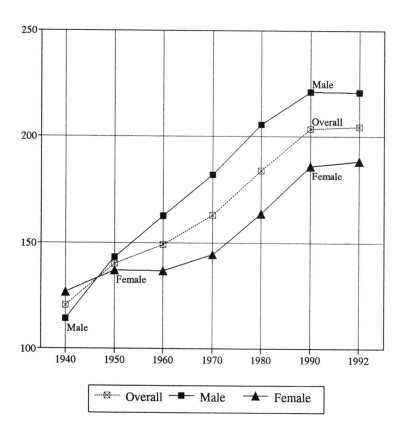

Year	Overall	Male	Female	Ratio
1940	120.3	114.1	126.4	0.90
1950	139.8	142.9	136.8	1.04
1960	149.2	162.5	136.4	1.19
1970	162.8	182.1	144.4	1.26
1980	183.9	205.3	163.6	1.25
1990	203.2	221.3	186.0	1.19
1992	204.3	220.8	188.2	1.17

Increases from 1940 through 1992:

Overall	69.8%
Male	93.5%
Female	48.9%

Figure 4-3 shows age-adjusted cancer death rates per 100,000 for the overall population and for males and females from 1960 through 1990. The exact rates are shown numerically in the table under the graph. The table also shows the ratio of the rate for males to the rate for females, as well as the increases from 1960 through 1990 of the three rates shown in the graph and the ratio of male rates to female rates. The age-adjusted reference year is 1940. The text accompanying Figure 2-1 explains the use of age-adjusted data and the significance of the reference year.

At the starting point of 1960, the male cancer death rate was 29 percent higher than the female cancer death rate, as shown by the ratio of 1.29 for 1960. The ratio increased from 1960 through 1980, then decreased slightly after 1980. From 1960 through 1990 the ratio increased by 14.7 percent. This is much different than the results of Figure 4-2 which used raw data. In Figure 4-2 the ratio was unchanged between 1960 and 1990.

In Figure 4-3, the overall cancer rate increased by 7.3 percent from 1960 through 1990, while the male rate increase by 16.3 percent and the female rate increased by 1.3 percent. The increases for the same period using the raw data of Figure 4-2 were 36.2 percent for the overall rate, exactly the same 36.2 percent for the male rate, and 36.4 percent for the female rate. Thus the age-adjusted data show the cancer death rate for females was almost constant from 1960 through 1990, compared to a 36.4 increase in the raw data. If not for lung cancer, the overall age-adjusted cancer death rate for females would have fallen from 1960 through 1990. Similarly, the age-adjusted male cancer death rate increased by only 16.3 percent rather than the 36.2 percent rate shown by the raw data. Lung cancer accounted for most of this increase as well.

The substantial differences in the results using age-adjusted data compared to raw data means that in the rest of Part IV only age-adjusted data will be used to make comparisons. The only exception will be the comparisons of death rates for selected age brackets in the male and female populations. As explained in the text accompanying Figure 3-4, using results from the same age brackets in the male and female populations eliminates problems due to the different age distributions of the male and female populations.

Further, even when using age-adjusted data, it is not possible to understand the differences in cancer death rates over time and/or between males and females without knowing the differences in cancer death rates by site. It is only when the cancer death rates by site are known that steps can be taken to prevent premature death due to cancer. Cancer can be "cured" by finding it before it metastasizes and removing it from the body. However, cancers grow and metastasize at different rates in different sites, and finding the cancer before it metastasizes is far more difficult in some sites than others. Thus, site information is crucial. Figure 4-4 begins the examination of cancer by site.

Figure 4-3. Male/Female Age-Adjusted Cancer Death Rates

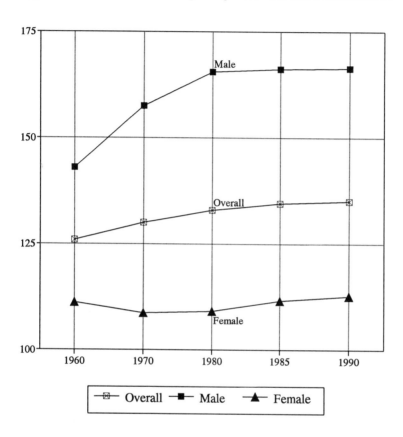

Year	Overall	Male	Female	Ratio
1960	125.8	143.0	111.2	1.29
1970	129.9	157.4	108.8	1.45
1980	132.8	165.5	109.2	1.52
1985	134.4	166.1	111.7	1.49
1990	135.0	166.3	112.7	1.48

Increases from 1960 through 1990:

Overall	7.3%
Male	16.3%
Female	1.3%
Ratio	14.7%

Note: Age-adjusted reference year is 1940.

Figure 4-4 shows age-adjusted cancer death rates per 100,000 from 1930 through 1990 for males by different sites in the body. The sites are the stomach, the colon and the rectum (Colon/Rectal), the prostate, and the lungs. The exact rates are shown numerically in the table under the graph. The table also shows the change in rates for the four sites from 1940 through 1990. Because of the sharp changes from 1930 through 1940, 1940 is used as the base year for the changes to give a more accurate picture of the course of cancer in the second half of the century. Figure 4-4 is based on data made available to the public by the American Cancer Society. The age-adjusted reference year is 1970 because it is the reference year preferred by the Society. The text accompanying Figure 2-1 explains the use of age-adjusted data and the significance of the reference year.

Stomach cancer death rates fell by 79.3 percent from 1940 through 1990. The decline from 1930 through 1990 was 82.1 percent (rates fell by 89.2 percent for females and thus the decline was independent of gender). It is believed the primary reason for the decrease was the great reduction in the use of salt-cured and smoked foods due to modernization of the methods used to process and preserve food. This is an excellent example of how death rates due to cancer can be affected by changes in our cultural environment.

Death rates due to cancer of the colon and rectum fell by 12.6 percent from 1940 through 1990, with most of the decrease taking place in the last decade. The key is early detection of the cancer so it can be removed surgically before it metastasizes. Stool blood tests, digital rectal examinations, and use of a hollow lighted tube (sigmoidoscope) to examine the colon are the prime methods of early detection. This reinforces the need for regular check-ups, especially as we age.

The death rate for prostate cancer increased by 24.5 percent from 1940 through 1990, with a large part of the increase taking place in the last decade. Once again the key is early detection to permit surgical removal before the cancer metastasizes. The recent development of a blood test (PSA) for prostate cancer, in addition to the standard digital examination, should lead to earlier detection and a reduction in the death rate. Prostate cancer usually grows slowly, especially in older men. This helps in its detection before it metastasizes, and in some cases the cancer can be left in place because an older man is likely to die of something else long before the cancer metastasizes.

The real horror story in cancer is the increase in the death rate from lung cancer. It grew by 567 percent between 1940 and 1990 (the increase is over 1400 percent since 1930). Lung cancer is directly tied to smoking (90 percent of lung cancer victims are smokers), and it is especially deadly because by the time it can be found it usually has already metastasized (often to the brain where it produces an exceptionally ugly death). Lung cancer kills 87 percent of its victims in less than five years after it is diagnosed. Never smoking or stopping smoking soon enough is the only "cure" because that prevents the cancer from starting.

Figure 4-4. Male Age-Adjusted Cancer Death Rates by Site

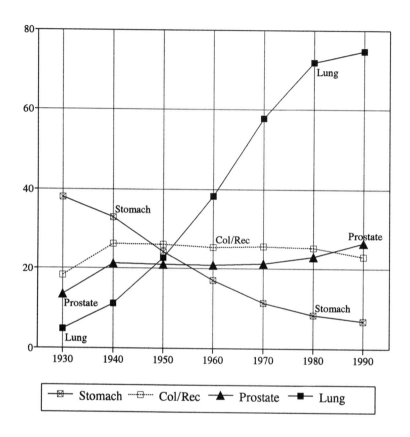

Year	Stomach	Colon/Rectal	Prostate	Lung
1930	38.0	18.3	13.6	4.9
1940	32.9	26.2	21.2	11.2
1950	24.2	26.0	21.0	22.6
1960	17.0	25.3	20.8	38.2
1970	11.4	25.6	21.2	57.7
1980	8.3	25.2	22.9	71.9
1990	6.8	22.9	26.4	74.7

Changes from 1940 through 1990:

Stomach	-79.3%	Prostate	24.5%
Col/Rectal	-12.6%	Lung	567%

Note: Age-adjusted reference year is 1970.

Figure 4-5 shows age-adjusted cancer death rates per 100,000 from 1930 through 1990 for females by different sites in the body. The sites are the uterus, the colon and the rectum (Colon/Rectal), the breasts, and the lungs. The exact rates are shown numerically in the table under the graph. The table also shows the change in rates for the four sites from 1940 through 1990. Because of the different changes from 1930 through 1940, 1940 is used as the base year for the changes to give a more accurate picture of the course of cancer in the second half of the century. Figure 4-5 is based on data made available to the public by the American Cancer Society. The age-adjusted reference year is 1970 because it is the reference year preferred by the Society. The text accompanying Figure 2-1 explains the use of age-adjusted data and the significance of the reference year.

Uterine cancer death rates fell by 81.8 percent from 1940 through 1990. The decline from 1930 through 1990 was 83.3 percent. This dramatic decline is the result of the "Pap" test, a test developed by Dr. George Papanicolaou in the 1940s. The test permits early detection of uterine cancer, allowing it to be surgically removed before it metastasizes. It was the decline of uterine cancer from the number one killer for women to a relatively minor problem that drove the overall cancer death rate for women below that of men (Figure 4-2).

Death rates due to cancer of the colon and rectum fell by 40.7 percent from 1940 through 1990. This is much greater than the decline for men (Figure 4-4), and since the key is early detection of the cancer so it can be removed surgically before it metastasizes, the probable cause of the greater drop in women is that they are more likely to have regular medical examinations than men. Stool blood tests, digital rectal examinations, and use of a hollow lighted tube (sigmoidoscope) to examine the colon are the prime methods of early detection.

The death rate for breast cancer declined by 3.6 percent from 1940 through 1990. Once again the key is early detection to permit surgical removal before the cancer metastasizes. The emphasis on self-examination education and advances in mammography that detects breast cancer at an early stage using X-rays have probably not only helped achieved the reduction, but also prevented an increase due to increases in the amount of fat in the diets of women. Breast cancer has received more publicity than any other kind of cancer in women, but the sad fact is that lung cancer now kills more women than breast cancer.

As women increased their level of smoking, the death rate for lung cancer increased sharply. It grew by 864 percent between 1940 and 1990 (the increase is nearly 1300 percent since 1930). The absolute rate is still below that of men (Figure 4-4), but lung cancer is now increasing more rapidly in women than in men, as women continue to smoke in large numbers in spite of the knowledge that smoking produces lung cancer. Since lung cancer usually has already metastasized by the time it is found, never smoking or stopping smoking soon enough is the only "cure" because that prevents the cancer from starting.

Figure 4-5. Female Age-Adjusted Cancer Death Rates by Site

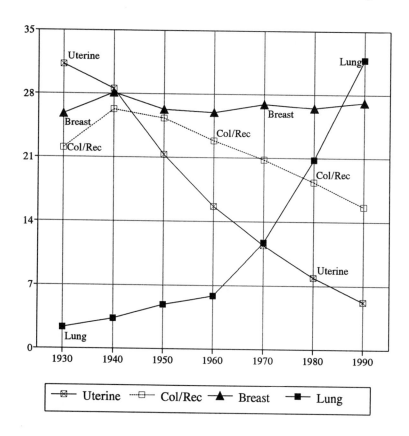

Year	Uterine	Colon/Rectal	Breast	Lung
1930	31.2	22.0	25.8	2.3
1940	28.5	26.3	28.1	3.3
1950	21.3	25.3	26.3	4.8
1960	15.6	22.8	26.0	5.8
1970	11.4	20.8	26.9	11.7
1980	7.9	18.3	26.5	20.8
1990	5.2	15.6	27.1	31.8

Changes from 1940 through 1990:

Uterine	-81.8%	Breast	-3.6%
Col/Rectal	-40.7%	Lung	864%

Note: Age-adjusted reference year is 1970.

Figure 4-6 shows age-adjusted cancer death rates per 100,000 from 1930 through 1990 for males and females in two categories. The first category is lung cancer, and the second is all other cancer. The exact rates are shown numerically in the table under the graph. The table also shows the change in rates for the two categories from 1940 through 1990. Using 1940 as the base year for the changes gives a more accurate picture of the course of cancer in the second half of the century, and it permits direct comparison with the same baseline used in Figures 4-4 and 4-5. Figure 4-6 is based on data made available to the public by the American Cancer Society. The age-adjusted reference year is 1970 because it is the reference year preferred by the Society. The text accompanying Figure 2-1 explains the use of age-adjusted data and the significance of the reference year.

The death rate for all cancers in males other than lung cancer fell steadily after 1940. The decline was 23.3 percent from 1940 through 1990. However, over the same period the death rate for lung cancer in males increased by 567 percent. This meant that by 1980 the death rate due to lung cancer in men was higher than the death rate of all other cancers put together. The gap increased in 1990, with the lung cancer death rate growing to 13 percent more than the combined death rate for all other cancers. However, the rate of increase in the lung cancer death rate from 1980 through 1990 was only 3.9 percent, the lowest increase in any decade since the starting point of 1930. This means that males have reduced their rate of smoking to the point that the lung cancer death rate has at least begun to show signs that it may soon stop increasing.

The death rate for all cancers in females other than lung cancer also fell steadily after 1940, just as in men. Thanks to the large reduction in uterine cancer (Figure 4-5), all other cancer in women declined by 51.1 percent from 1940 through 1990, more than twice the decline recorded for all other cancer in men. The death rate for lung cancer in females was just under half the rate for men in 1930 (the male to female ratio was 2.1). But as the effects of long-term smoking began to drive up the lung cancer death rate in men, the death rate for men soared to 6.6 times the rate for women by 1960. However, the lung cancer death rate for women began to climb sharply after 1960 in response to the much higher rate of smoking in women that started earlier in the century. By 1990 the ratio of the lung cancer death rate for men compared to that of women was 2.3, not far from where it had been in 1930.

In 1990, the death rate for all other cancer in women was 1.6 times as high as the death rate for lung cancer. But in 1930 it was 47 times as high. The 864 percent increase in the lung cancer death rate in women from 1940 through 1990 brought the two rates closer together, and lung cancer deaths in women may eventually exceed deaths from all other kinds of cancer, as is the case for men. The adoption of smoking on a large scale in the Twentieth Century, first by men and later by women, is truly an American tragedy.

Figure 4-6. Male/Female Age-Adjusted Cancer Rates by Site

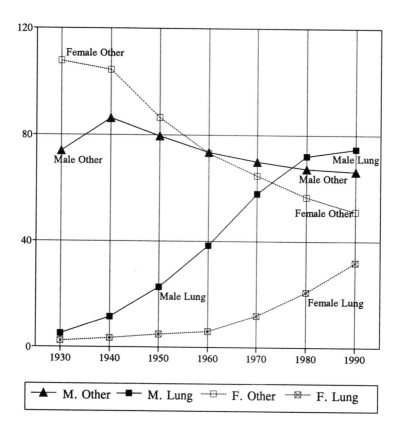

Year	Male Other and Lung Cancer		Female Other and Lung Cancer	
1930	73.7	4.9	107.6	2.3
1940	86.2	11.2	104.3	3.3
1950	79.5	22.6	86.4	4.8
1960	73.4	38.2	73.0	5.8
1970	69.7	57.7	64.6	11.7
1980	67.1	71.9	56.6	20.8
1990	66.1	74.7	51.0	31.8

Changes from 1940 through 1990:

Male Other	-23.3%	Female Other	-51.1%
Male Lung	567%	Female Lung	864%

Note: Age-adjusted reference year is 1970.

Figure 4-7 shows the variation from 1940 through 1992 of death rates per 100,000 for total cancer, respiratory cancer, and all other cancer for males in the 45-54 age bracket. Respiratory cancer includes lung cancer and other cancers in the respiratory tract, but the major component is lung cancer. The exact rates for each category are shown numerically in the table under the graph. The table also shows the ratio of the rate for all other cancer to the rate for respiratory cancer, as well as the percentage declines from 1940 through 1992 for each of the three death rates in the graph.

As discussed in the text accompanying Figure 3-4, comparing results for selected age brackets in different populations eliminates the problem of misleading comparisons due to different age distributions in the different populations. Thus, the rest of the figures in Part IV compare male and female results using selected age brackets in the male and female populations. This permits the data for the same age brackets to be compared directly.

The total cancer death rate for males in the 45-54 age bracket rose steadily from 1940 through 1980, and then declined by 18.5 percent from 1980 through 1992. This put the overall increase from 1940 through 1992 at 13.7 percent. All of the increase and most of the later decline were due to changes in the death rate for respiratory cancer.

The death rate for respiratory cancer increased by 148 percent from 1940 through 1992, but that includes a decline of 27.7 percent from 1980 through 1992. The increase in the respiratory cancer death rate from 1940 through 1980 was 242 percent. That reduced the ratio between the death rate for all other cancer and the death rate for respiratory cancer to 1.36 in 1980. This means that the death rate for all other cancer was only 36 percent higher than that for respiratory cancer in 1980, a dramatic reduction from 1940 when the ratio was 4.81, and the death rate for all other cancer was 381 percent higher than the death rate for respiratory cancer.

The death rate for all other cancer declined by 14.2 percent from 1940 through 1992. There was a small increase between 1940 and 1950, and then the death rate for all other cancer declined steadily from 1950 through 1992. Once again, the cancer death rate for men in the 45-54 age bracket would be a slowly declining problem if not for respiratory cancer. The reality is that there is not so much a cancer problem as there is a smoking problem in the United States.

Lung cancer is usually a slow growing cancer. It often takes decades of smoking before it produces symptoms. But by the time it produces symptoms it usually has already metastasized. This is a sentence of death. The good news is that if one quits smoking before lung cancer has developed, then it is just as if one never smoked at all from the perspective of lung cancer. This means it is never too late to stop. It is better not to smoke at all, but it is never too late to realize benefits from stopping.

Figure 4-7. Male Cancer Death Rates per 100,000 (Age 45-54)

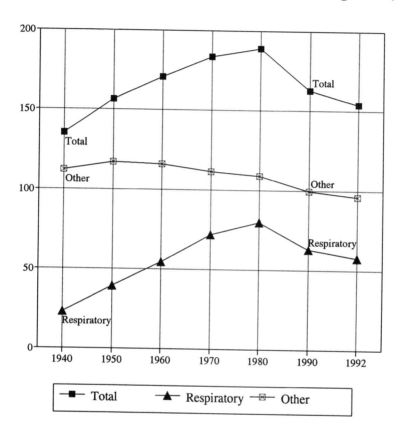

Year	Total	Respiratory	Other	Ratio
1940	135.3	23.3	112.0	4.81
1950	156.2	39.3	116.9	2.97
1960	170.8	54.7	116.1	2.12
1970	183.5	72.1	111.4	1.55
1980	188.7	79.8	108.9	1.36
1990	162.5	63.0	99.5	1.58
1992	153.8	57.7	96.1	1.67

Changes from 1940 through 1992:

Total	13.7%
Respiratory	148%
Other	-14.2%

Figure 4-8 shows the variation from 1940 through 1992 of death rates per 100,000 for total cancer, respiratory cancer, and all other cancer for males in the 55-64 age bracket. Respiratory cancer includes lung cancer and other cancers in the respiratory tract, but the major component is lung cancer. The exact rates for each category are shown numerically in the table under the graph. The table also shows the ratio of the rate for all other cancer to the rate for respiratory cancer, as well as the percentage declines from 1940 through 1992 for each of the three death rates in the graph. Figure 4-7 shows similar data for males in the 45-54 age bracket.

The total cancer death rate for males in the 55-64 age bracket rose steadily from 1940 through 1990, and then declined by 3.7 percent from 1990 through 1992. This put the overall increase from 1940 through 1992 at 45.8 percent. All of the increase and most of the later decline were due to changes in the death rate for respiratory cancer.

The death rate for respiratory cancer increased by 375 percent from 1940 through 1992, but that includes a decline of 6.7 percent from 1990 through 1992. The increase in the respiratory cancer death rate from 1940 through 1990 was 409 percent. That reduced the ratio between the death rate for all other cancer and the death rate for respiratory cancer to 1.29 in 1990. This means the death rate for all other cancer was only 29 percent higher than that for respiratory cancer in 1990, a dramatic reduction from 1940 when the ratio was 6.71, and the death rate for all other cancer was 571 percent higher than the death rate for respiratory cancer.

The death rate for all other cancer declined by 3.3 percent from 1940 through 1992. There was a small increase between 1940 and 1950, and then the death rate for all other cancer declined steadily from 1950 through 1980 before small changes up and down occurred in 1990 and 1992 respectively. The death rate for all other cancer for men in the 55-64 age bracket was about three times as high as that for the 45-54 age bracket (Figure 4-7), but the variations over time were quite similar.

However, the death rate for respiratory cancer in the 55-64 age bracket was 3.8 times as high as in the 45-54 bracket in 1992, after being less than twice as high in 1940. This increase in ratio was due to the long time it takes for lung cancer to develop and grow. This means that the ratio between the death rate for all other cancer and that for respiratory cancer was much lower in 1990 and 1992 in the 55-64 age bracket than in the 45-54 age bracket. As men age, the death rate for respiratory cancer comes closer and closer to the total death rate for all other cancer. Lung cancer is the great killer.

Figures 4-9 and 4-10 show results for females in the 45-54 and 55-64 age brackets respectively. As discussed in the text accompanying Figure 4-7, using the same age brackets permits direct comparison of male and female results.

Figure 4-8. Male Cancer Death Rates per 100,000 (Age 55-64)

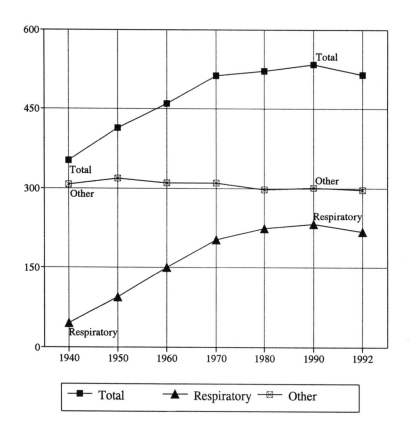

Year	Total	Respiratory	Other	Ratio
1940	352.2	45.7	306.5	6.71
1950	413.1	94.2	318.9	3.39
1960	459.9	150.2	309.7	2.06
1970	511.8	202.3	309.5	1.53
1980	520.8	223.8	297.0	1.33
1990	532.9	232.6	300.3	1.29
1992	513.4	217.0	296.4	1.37

Changes from 1940 through 1992:

Total	45.8%	
Respiratory	375%	
Other	-3.3%	

Figure 4-9 shows the variation from 1940 through 1992 of death rates per 100,000 for total cancer, respiratory cancer, and all other cancer for females in the 45-54 age bracket. Respiratory cancer includes lung cancer and other cancers in the respiratory tract, but the major component is lung cancer. The exact rates for each category are shown numerically in the table under the graph. The table also shows the ratio of the rate for all other cancer to the rate for respiratory cancer, as well as the percentage declines from 1940 through 1992 for each of the three death rates in the graph.

The total cancer death rate for females in the 45-54 age bracket fell steadily from 1940 through 1992, declining by 28.0 percent during the period. This is the reverse of the case for males where the total cancer death rate increased by 13.7 percent from 1940 through 1992 (Figure 4-7). From 1940 through 1980, the total rate for females decreased by 15.8 percent, while the total rate for males increased by 39.5 percent. The difference was due to the fact that uterine cancer fell sharply for females (Figure 4-5), while respiratory cancer was rising sharply for males (Figure 4-7).

The death rate for respiratory cancer for females increased by 424 percent from 1940 through 1992, but that includes a decline of 7.9 percent from 1990 through 1992. The increase in the respiratory cancer death rate from 1940 through 1990 was 469 percent. That reduced the ratio between the death rate for all other cancer and the death rate for respiratory cancer to 3.41 in 1990. This means the death rate for respiratory cancer was only 22.7 percent of the total cancer death rate for females in the 45-54 age bracket in 1990, but that was a dramatic increase from only 3.0 percent in 1940 when the ratio was 31.9.

The death rate for all other cancer declined by 42.1 percent from 1940 through 1992 due to the drop in uterine cancer as discussed above. This was a much larger decline than the 14.2 percent decline for males in the 45-54 age bracket over the same period (Figure 4-7). The death rate for all other cancer for females in 1940 was 76.7 percent higher than for men. By 1992, the death rate for all other cancer in females was only 19.1 percent higher than in men. This is one of the few areas where men have a lower death rate than women. But the key point is that the death rate for all other cancers declined for both males and females. Cancer was a declining threat from 1940 through 1992 for both males and females except for the surge in lung cancer.

In the 45-54 age bracket, the death rate for respiratory cancer for females was 73.4 percent below that for males in 1940. By 1992, the female death rate for respiratory cancer was 43.7 percent below that for males. Unfortunately, this gap will probably continue to close. This means that the total cancer death rate for women in the 45-54 age bracket may once again be higher than that for males in the same bracket, as it was from 1940 through 1960. In 1992 the total cancer death rate for males was only 4.4 percent above that for females.

Figure 4-9. Female Cancer Death Rates per 100,000 (Age 45-54)

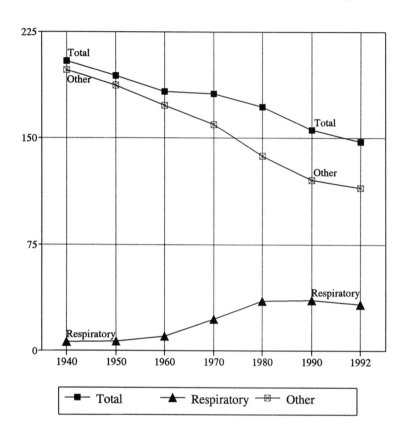

Year	Total	Respiratory	Other	Ratio
1940	204.1	6.2	197.9	31.9
1950	194.0	6.7	187.3	28.0
1960	183.0	10.1	172.9	17.1
1970	181.5	22.2	159.3	7.18
1980	171.8	34.8	137.0	3.94
1990	155.5	35.3	120.2	3.41
1992	147.0	32.5	114.5	3.52

Changes from 1940 through 1992:

Total	-28.0%
Respiratory	424%
Other	-42.1%

Figure 4-10 shows the variation from 1940 through 1992 of death rates per 100,000 for total cancer, respiratory cancer, and all other cancer for females in the 55-64 age bracket. Respiratory cancer includes lung cancer and other cancers in the respiratory tract, but the major component is lung cancer. The exact rates for each category are shown numerically in the table under the graph. The table also shows the ratio of the rate for all other cancer to the rate for respiratory cancer, as well as the percentage declines from 1940 through 1992 for each of the three death rates in the graph.

The total cancer death rate for females in the 55-64 bracket fell from 1940 through 1960, then increased from 1960 through 1990 before falling slightly from 1990 through 1992. Overall, the death rate declined by 3.7 percent from 1940 through 1992. This is quite different from the case for females in the 45-54 age group where the total death rate steadily declined from 1940 through 1992 (Figure 4-9), producing a total decline of 28.0 percent from 1940 through 1992. The main reason for the difference was the strong increase in the respiratory cancer death rate from 1940 through 1992 for females in the 55-64 age bracket.

The death rate for respiratory cancer for females in the 55-64 age bracket increased by 760 percent from 1940 through 1992. It was only 2.0 times as high as the rate for the 45-54 age bracket in 1940, but by 1992 the death rate for the 55-64 bracket was 3.3 times as high as for the 45-54 bracket. The ratio between the death rate for all other cancer and the death rate for respiratory cancer was 2.41 in 1990, meaning that the death rate for respiratory cancer was 29.3 percent of the total cancer death rate for females in the 55-64 bracket in 1992, a dramatic increase from only 3.3 percent in 1940 when the ratio was 29.5.

The death rate for all other cancer in females in the 55-64 age bracket declined by 29.7 percent from 1940 through 1992, and the decline was reasonably consistent during the period. The death rate for all other cancer for females in 1940 was 21.2 percent higher than that for males in the same age bracket (Figure 4-8). By 1992, the death rate for all other cancer in females was 11.8 percent below the corresponding death rate in males. Cancer was a steady declining problem for females in the 55-64 bracket from 1940 through 1992 except for the huge rise in deaths from lung cancer.

The death rate for respiratory cancer for females in the 55-64 age bracket was 72.4 percent below that for males in 1940. By 1992, the female death rate for respiratory cancer was exactly 50 percent of that for males. The percentages in these comparisons are quite similar to those for the 45-64 age bracket. Females continue to catch up to males in the respiratory cancer death rate at all ages even as males at higher ages increase their death rate margins compared to females for total cancer.

Figure 4-11 demonstrates this increasing margin with age by showing male and female total cancer death rates for six different age brackets.

Figure 4-10. Female Cancer Death Rates per 100,000 (Age 55-64)

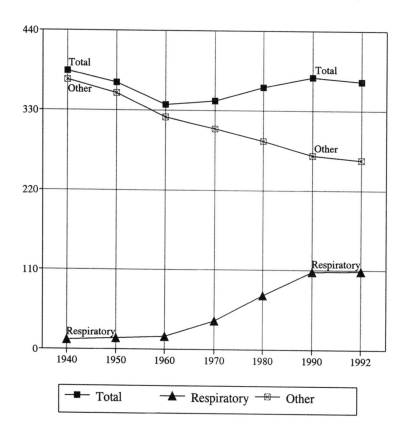

Year	Total	Respiratory	Other	Ratio
1940	384.1	12.6	371.5	29.5
1950	368.2	15.4	352.8	22.9
1960	337.7	17.0	320.7	18.9
1970	343.2	38.9	304.3	7.82
1980	361.7	74.5	287.2	3.86
1990	375.2	107.6	267.6	2.49
1992	369.7	108.4	261.3	2.41

Changes from 1940 through 1992:

Total	-3.7%
Respiratory	760%
Other	-29.7%

Figure 4-11 shows cancer death rates per 100,000 for the overall population and for males and females in six age brackets. The brackets are 35-44, 45-54, 55-64, 65-74, 75-84, and 85 up. The exact rates are shown numerically in the table under the graph. The table also shows the ratio of the cancer death rates for males to those for females, as well as the ratio for all of the measures at age 85 up compared to the 35-44 age bracket.

At all ages except the 35-44 age bracket, the cancer death rate for males is higher than that for females. The margin increases steadily with age as shown by the ratio between males and females increasing from 0.82 in the 35-44 age bracket to 2.01 for the 85 up bracket. This means that males had a death rate 18.1 percent below females in the 35-44 bracket, while they had a rate 101 percent higher than females in the 85 up bracket. Similarly, in the 35-44 bracket, the rate for males was 9.9 percent below the overall rate, while the rate for females was 9.9 percent above. But in the 85 up bracket, males were 56.8 percent above the overall rate, while females were 22.0 percent below.

Regardless of gender, Figure 4-11 shows clearly how the death rate for cancer increases sharply with age. Because males have a lower rate in the 35-44 age bracket, the increase for males between the 35-44 bracket and the 85 up bracket is much more than that for females. This is shown by the ratios at the bottom of the table. The overall rate is 42.3 times higher in the 85 up bracket than in the 35-44 bracket. For males the rate in the 85 up bracket is 73.6 times as high as in the 35-44 bracket, while for females the rate in the 85 up bracket is 30.0 times as high as in the 35-44 bracket. The ratio between males and females in the 85 up bracket is 2.5 times as high as in the 35-44 bracket.

If there were an equal number of males and females in each age bracket, the overall death rate would be the average between the male and female rates. But for brackets above age 45, the overall rate is always less than the average between the male and female rates, and the female rate is lower than the male rate. This means there must more females in each age bracket. This is another measure of the fact that women live longer than men at all ages. But unlike heart disease (Figure 3-9), more men die of cancer than women because the death rate margin for men is so high at the higher ages. For example, above the age of 65, the number of deaths due to cancer for men is about 12 percent higher than that for women.

The key message about cancer death rates in all of the different ways it was measured in Part IV was that cancer would be a declining problem if not for the huge increase in lung cancer deaths. Thus, the key to preventing premature death due to cancer is to never smoke or to stop immediately. Quitting or avoiding smoking also can help prevent premature death in other ways, and there are a series of relatively simple steps that can be taken to prevent premature death due to causes other than cancer. These steps are discussed in detail in Part V.

Figure 4-11. Male/Female Cancer Death Rates/100,000 by Age

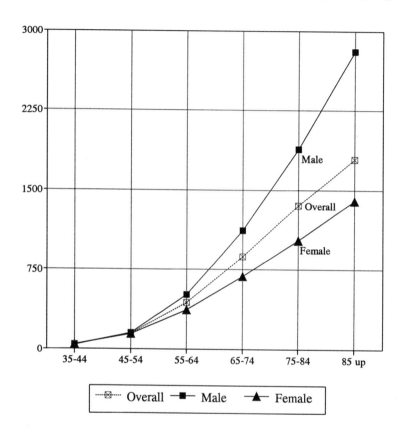

Age	Overall	Male	Female	Ratio
35-44	42.3	38.1	46.5	0.82
45-54	150.3	153.8	147.0	1.05
55-64	437.8	513.4	369.7	1.39
65-74	873.4	1111.1	686.5	1.62
75-84	1350.9	1882.7	1025.6	1.84
85 up	1787.3	2802.3	1393.9	2.01

Increase at 85 up compared to 35-44 (ratio):

Overall	42.3
Male	73.6
Female	30.0
Ratio	2.5

Part V
The Future

The Killers in Our Future

Table 5-1 shows the leading causes of death for the overall population for different age brackets. The top six causes are shown through age 44 and the top seven causes above age 45. The figures are from 1992, the last year for which complete data are available. But changes in the leading causes of death occur very slowly, and the data in Table 5-1 can be considered current today. The age brackets include all ages from 1 to 65 up. The table shows the death rate per 100,000 and the percentage of total deaths resulting from each cause. It also shows the percentage of total deaths included in the leading causes, the total death rate for the specific age bracket, and the ratio of the death rate in the age bracket to the death rate for people at all ages (footnote two).

The leading causes of death in the future for most of us are those that apply to people older than we are today. We look into the future by learning what is happening in the age bracket we move into next. Tables 5-2 and 5-3 show results for males and females respectively for the age brackets used in Table 5-1. Table 5-4 shows results for males and females for age brackets above age 65.

As discussed in the text accompanying Figure 2-4, the first year of life is a very dangerous year and deaths are much higher in that year than in subsequent decades. Thus, the first age bracket in Table 5-1 is the 1-4 age bracket. The leading cause of death is accidents (as it is in the first four age brackets). The death rate for persons at all ages is 19.6 times as high as the death rate in the 1-4 age bracket. Accidents are the leading cause of death in the 5-14 age bracket, and in the 15-24 age bracket violent deaths (accidents, homicide, and suicide) occupy the top three places and account for 76.3 percent of all deaths in the bracket.

Accidents also top the 25-44 age bracket, and it is not until age 45 that systemic problems in the body take over the top spots. But even in the 45-64 age bracket, cancer causes more deaths than heart disease (as it does in every age bracket up to age 65). In spite of the fact that since 1930 heart disease has easily been the biggest killer in the general population (Tables 2-1 and 2-2), it does not become the leading cause of death until after age 65.

There are substantial differences in the leading causes of death for males and females in every age bracket, and thus it is necessary to review the leading causes of death by gender to determine the future leading causes of death for each individual. This review begins with Figure 5-2, which shows the leading causes of death for males in each age bracket.

Table 5-1. Leading Causes of Death at Different Ages

Cause of Death	Rate	% of Total	Cause of Death	Rate	% of Total
Age 1-4			**Age 5-14**		
Accidents	15.9	36.5%	Accidents	9.3	41.3%
Congenital[1]	5.5	12.6%	Cancer	3.0	13.3%
Cancer	3.1	7.1%	Homicide	1.6	7.1%
Homicide	2.8	6.4%	Congenital	1.2	5.3%
Heart Disease	1.8	4.1%	Heart Disease	0.8	3.6%
Pneumonia/Flu	1.2	2.8%	Pneumonia/Flu	0.3	1.3%
Top Six Causes	30.3	69.5%	Top Six Causes	16.2	72.0%
Total Age 1-4	43.6		Total Age 5-14	22.5	
Ratio to All Ages:[2] 19.6			Ratio to All Ages: 37.9		
Age 15-24			**Age 25-44**		
Accidents	37.8	39.5%	Accidents	31.3	17.2%
Homicide	22.2	23.2%	HIV/AIDS	29.9	16.4%
Suicide	13.0	13.6%	Cancer	26.9	14.8%
Cancer	5.0	5.2%	Heart Disease	19.6	10.8%
Heart Disease	2.7	2.8%	Suicide	14.8	8.1%
HIV/AIDS[3]	1.6	1.7%	Homicide	14.3	7.9%
Top Six Causes	82.3	86.1%	Top Six Causes	136.8	75.2%
Total Age 15-24	95.6		Total Age 25-44	181.9	
Ratio to All Ages: 8.9			Ratio to All Ages: 4.7		
Age 45-64			**Age 65 up**		
Cancer	274.7	36.3%	Heart Disease	1844.5	37.8%
Heart Disease	215.0	28.4%	Cancer	1121.8	23.0%
Stroke	30.0	4.0%	Stroke	388.5	8.0%
Accidents	28.7	3.8%	COPD	242.2	5.0%
COPD[4]	25.6	3.4%	Pneumonia/Flu	209.1	4.3%
Liver Disease	21.4	2.8%	Diabetes	115.7	2.4%
Diabetes	21.3	2.8%	Accidents	82.5	1.7%
Top Seven Causes	616.7	81.4%	Top Seven Causes	4004.3	82.0%
Total Age 45-64	757.2		Total Age 65 up	4880.6	
Ratio to All Ages: 1.1			Ratio to All Ages: 5.7		

1--Congenital deaths are due to problems existing at birth.

2--Ratio to All Ages is the ratio of the overall death rate at all ages to the death rate for the specific age group being considered. The overall death rate is 852.9 and in this case is 19.6 times higher than that of the Age 1-4 group. For Age 65 up, the ratio is reversed.

3--HIV is the human immunodeficiency virus that causes AIDS (acquired immunodeficiency syndrome).

4--COPD (chronic obstructive pulmonary diseases) includes bronchitis, emphysema, and asthma.

Table 5-2 shows the leading causes of death for males in different age brackets. The top six causes are shown through age 44 and the top seven causes above age 45. The age brackets include all ages from 1 to 65 up. The table shows the death rate per 100,000 and the percentage of total deaths resulting from each cause. It also shows the percentage of total deaths included in the leading causes, the total death rate for the specific age bracket, and the ratio of the death rate in the age bracket to the death rate for males at all ages (footnote two). The text accompanying Table 5-1 explains how Table 5-2 permits males to look into the future regarding the expected causes of death, and why the table begins with age one rather than birth.

For males, accidents are the leading cause of death in the first three age brackets, as is true for both the overall population and for females. But males have much higher accident rates in all three brackets. As car insurance companies can confirm, the accident rate for males is nearly three times as high as that for females in the 15-24 age bracket (Figure 5-3). But the rate for males is 51.6 percent higher than that for females in the 1-4 age bracket, and 96.8 percent higher in the 5-14 age bracket. Even though accidents are no longer the leading cause of death for males above age 24, their rate is substantially higher than that for females in all age brackets. At all stages of life, males clearly are more inclined than females to put themselves in situations where accidents occur.

HIV/AIDS is the leading cause of death for males in the 25-44 age bracket, followed closely by accidents. Above age 44, heart disease becomes the leading killer for males. The male death rate for heart disease is 2.6 times as high as that for females in the 45-64 age bracket, and 23 percent higher than that for females in age 65 up bracket. But cancer is a very close second in the 45-64 bracket for males. This is because lung cancer kills enough males before heart disease reaches the deadly stage to make cancer a strong competitor below age 65.

Before age 45 the leading causes of death in males are highly preventable. Accidents can be considered a matter of bad luck, but the fact that the male rate is so much higher than the female rate even at ages below 15 implies that males are simply more reckless. HIV/AIDS is clearly a preventable disease now that so much is known about its method of transmission. For males who do not engage in unsafe sex and do not use drugs, HIV/AIDS is not a problem. But even with such problems, the total number of deaths below age 45 is not very large. As shown by the ratios below each age bracket, the overall death rate for males is much higher than that for each bracket until the 45-64 bracket.

The death rate in the 45-64 age bracket for males is nearly the same as for males at all ages (ratio of 0.9). The next bracket (65 up) has a death rate 6.3 times higher than that of males at all ages. This means that the causes of death above age 65 are the most important causes to consider to prevent premature death. Figure 5-4 provides much more detail for brackets above age 65.

Table 5-2. Male Leading Causes of Death at Different Ages

Cause of Death	Rate	% of Total
Age 1-4		
Accidents	19.1	39.8%
Congenital[1]	5.8	12.1%
Cancer	3.1	6.5%
Homicide	3.0	6.3%
Heart Disease	1.9	4.0%
Pneumonia/Flu	1.2	2.5%
Top Six Causes	34.1	71.0%
Total Age 1-4	48.0	
Ratio to All Ages:[2] 18.8		

Cause of Death	Rate	% of Total
Age 5-14		
Accidents	12.2	44.9%
Cancer	3.4	12.5%
Homicide	2.0	7.4%
Congenital	1.3	4.8%
Heart Disease	0.9	3.3%
Pneumonia/Flu	0.3	1.1%
Top Six Causes	20.1	73.9%
Total Age 5-14	27.2	
Ratio to All Ages: 33.1		

Cause of Death	Rate	% of Total
Age 15-24		
Accidents	55.5	39.1%
Homicide	37.3	26.3%
Suicide	21.9	15.4%
Cancer	5.9	4.2%
Heart Disease	3.4	2.4%
HIV/AIDS[3]	2.3	1.6%
Top Six Causes	126.3	89.1%
Total Age 15-24	141.8	
Ratio to All Ages: 6.4		

Cause of Death	Rate	% of Total
Age 25-44		
HIV/AIDS	52.5	20.3%
Accidents	48.7	18.9%
Heart Disease	28.6	11.1%
Cancer	24.6	9.5%
Suicide	23.9	9.3%
Homicide	22.7	8.8%
Top Six Causes	201.0	77.8%
Total Age 25-44	258.3	
Ratio to All Ages: 3.5		

Cause of Death	Rate	% of Total
Age 45-64		
Heart Disease	314.1	36.3%
Cancer	306.7	28.4%
Accidents	42.6	4.0%
Stroke	33.7	3.8%
Liver Disease	31.3	3.4%
COPD[4]	29.0	2.8%
Diabetes	23.0	2.8%
Top Seven Causes	780.4	81.4%
Total Age 45-64	970.1	
Ratio to All Ages: 0.9		

Cause of Death	Rate	% of Total
Age 65 up		
Heart Disease	2079.6	36.9%
Cancer	1466.1	26.0%
Stroke	358.3	6.4%
COPD	329.4	5.8%
Pneumonia/Flu	232.9	4.1%
Diabetes	114.0	2.0%
Accidents	102.3	1.8%
Top Seven Causes	4682.6	83.1%
Total Age 65 up	5638.1	
Ratio to All Ages: 6.3		

1--Congenital deaths are due to problems existing at birth.

2--Ratio to All Ages is the ratio of the overall death rate at all ages to the death rate for the specific age group being considered. The overall death rate is 901.6 and in this case is 18.8 times higher than that of the Age 1-4 group. For Age 65 up the ratio is reversed.

3--HIV is the human immunodeficiency virus that causes AIDS (acquired immunodeficiency syndrome).

4--COPD (chronic obstructive pulmonary diseases) includes bronchitis, emphysema, and asthma.

Table 5-3 shows the leading causes of death for females in different age brackets. The top six causes are shown through age 44 and the top seven causes above age 45. The age brackets include all ages from 1 to 65 up. The table shows the death rate per 100,000 and the percentage of total deaths resulting from each cause. It also shows the percentage of total deaths included in the leading causes, the total death rate for the specific age bracket, and the ratio of the death rate in the age bracket to the death rate for females at all ages (footnote two). The text accompanying Table 5-1 explains how Table 5-2 permits females to look into the future regarding the expected causes of death, and why the table begins with age one rather than birth.

For females, accidents are the leading cause of death in the first three age brackets, as is true for both the overall population and for males (Table 5-2). But females have much lower accident rates in all three brackets. Accidents are the leading cause of death for females in these brackets because no other cause produces many deaths. Thus, even though the accident rate is much lower than that for males, it still is the leading cause of death for females.

Cancer becomes the leading cause of death for females in the 25-44 age bracket, and the death rate for cancer is more than twice as high as that for accidents, which are in second place. Cancer is also the leading cause of death in the 45-64 age bracket, and it also has a death rate nearly twice as high as the cause in second place (heart disease). But the cancer death rate for females in the 45-64 bracket is still 20.1 percent below that for males in the 45-64 bracket, even though cancer is only the second leading cause of death for males in the bracket. Once again, the overall female death rate is low enough that cancer causes a high percentage of total deaths even thought the absolute death rate is small on a relative basis. This is more evidence that females are less likely to die than males at all ages, especially before menopause.

While the leading causes of death in males before age 45 are highly preventable (Table 5-1), the same is not true for females. Their accident death rate is much lower than that for males, and the female death rate for HIV/AIDS is 85.7 percent below that for males in the 25-44 age bracket. Further, while the death rate for the 45-64 bracket for males is about 7 percent higher than that for all ages, the death rate for the 45-64 bracket for females is 31 percent lower than the death rate for all ages. However, stopping smoking to stop lung cancer is one step that would help cut the female death rate before age 65.

The death rate in the 65 up bracket for females is 5.4 times as high as the death rate for all ages. This is the first bracket in which the bracket death rate is higher than the overall rate. Heart disease is the leading cause of death for females in the 65 up bracket, and the death rate for heart disease is nearly twice as high as that for cancer in second place. Preventing premature death requires focusing on the 65 up bracket. Table 5-4 shows results in detail above age 65.

Table 5-3. Female Leading Causes of Death at Different Ages

Cause of Death	Rate	% of Total	Cause of Death	Rate	% of Total
Age 1-4			**Age 5-14**		
Accidents	12.6	32.3%	Accidents	6.2	35.4%
Congenital[1]	5.2	13.3%	Cancer	2.6	14.9%
Cancer	3.0	7.7%	Homicide	1.2	6.9%
Homicide	2.5	6.4%	Congenital	1.2	6.9%
Heart Disease	1.8	4.6%	Heart Disease	0.7	4.0%
Pneumonia/Flu	1.2	3.1%	Pneumonia/Flu	0.3	1.7%
Top Six Causes	26.3	67.4%	Top Six Causes	12.2	69.7%
Total Age 1-4	39.0		Total Age 5-14	17.5	
Ratio to All Ages:[2] 20.7			Ratio to All Ages: 33.1		
Age 15-24			**Age 25-44**		
Accidents	19.3	40.9%	Cancer	29.2	27.5%
Homicide	6.4	13.6%	Accidents	14.1	13.3%
Cancer	4.1	8.7%	Heart Disease	10.6	10.0%
Suicide	3.7	7.8%	HIV/AIDS	7.5	7.1%
Heart Disease	1.9	4.0%	Homicide	6.0	5.7%
HIV/AIDS[3]	0.9	1.9%	Suicide	5.8	5.5%
Top Six Causes	36.3	76.9%	Top Six Causes	73.2	69.0%
Total Age 15-24	47.2		Total Age 25-44	106.1	
Ratio to All Ages: 17.1			Ratio to All Ages: 7.6		
Age 45-64			**Age 65 up**		
Cancer	245.0	43.8%	Heart Disease	1685.1	38.6%
Heart Disease	122.7	22.0%	Cancer	888.3	20.3%
Stroke	26.5	4.7%	Stroke	409.0	9.4%
COPD[4]	22.5	4.0%	Pneumonia/Flu	193.0	4.4%
Diabetes	19.8	3.5%	COPD	183.1	4.2%
Accidents	15.8	2.8%	Diabetes	116.8	2.7%
Liver Disease	12.2	2.2%	Accidents	69.1	1.6%
Top Seven Causes	464.5	83.1%	Top Seven Causes	3544.4	81.2%
Total Age 45-64	558.8		Total Age 65 up	4366.9	
Ratio to All Ages: 1.4			Ratio to All Ages: 5.4		

1--Congenital deaths are due to problems existing at birth.

2--Ratio to All Ages is the ratio of the overall death rate at all ages to the death rate for the specific age group being considered. The overall death rate is 806.5 and in this case is 20.7 times higher than that of the Age 1-4 group. For Age 65 up the ratio is reversed.

3--HIV is the human immunodeficiency virus that causes AIDS (acquired immunodeficiency syndrome).

4--COPD (chronic obstructive pulmonary diseases) includes bronchitis, emphysema, and asthma.

Table 5-4 shows the top seven leading causes of death for males and females in different age brackets. The age brackets are 65-74, 75-84, and 85 up. The table shows the death rate per 100,000 and the percentage of total deaths resulting from each cause. It also shows the percentage of total deaths included in the top seven leading causes, the total death rate for the specific age bracket, and the ratio of the death rate in the age bracket to the death rate for males and females at all ages (footnote two). The table also shows the ratio of the results for males compared to those for females, and the ratios of the total death rate and its ratio to the death rate at all ages. The causes of death are listed in rank order for the 75-84 age bracket. This order is the same for males and females in that bracket, but not necessarily the same for all age brackets. Using this order permits the listing of causes to be the same in each category. The text accompanying Table 5-1 explains how Table 5-4 permits males and females to look into the future regarding the expected causes of death.

Heart disease is the leading cause of death for males in all age brackets, but cancer is still the leading cause for females in the 65-74 bracket. It is not until age 75 that heart disease becomes the leading cause of death for females. The ratios at the bottom of the table show that males have a higher death rate than females for all causes in all age brackets, with the exception of stroke in the 85 up age bracket. In this one case, females have a death rate six percent higher than that for males. Otherwise males lead in every possible category, with margins ranging from 7 percent to 162 percent.

Even for ages above 65, males have much higher death rates from accidents than females. Males lead females by 97.1 percent in the 65-74 bracket, 73.7 percent in the 75-84 bracket, and 56.4 percent in the 85 up bracket. In each case these ratios are much higher than the rate at which males lead females overall as shown by the ratios at the bottom of the table. There is no doubt that throughout life males are much more likely to suffer from accidents than females, as discussed in the text accompanying Table 5-2.

The ratio of the death rate for heart disease for males compared to females declines from 2.01 in the 65-74 bracket to 1.14 in the 85 up bracket. In this case the males finally reach near parity with females. But the cancer death rate ratio increases from 1.62 in the 65-74 bracket to 2.01 in the 85 up bracket. The only causes of death that might be considered as "female diseases" are stroke and diabetes. As noted, females have a higher death rate from stroke than males in the 85 up category, and the ratio for diabetes is near 1.0 in each age bracket. Although males still lead in each bracket, the ratio for diabetes is much lower than the ratio of the overall death rates for males and females.

Now that the leading causes of death in every age bracket are known, the key question is how to prevent premature death from these causes. Table 5-5 begins the process of showing how premature death can be prevented.

Table 5-4. Leading Causes of Death Above Age 65

Cause of Death	Rate	% of Total	Rate	% of Total	Rate	% of Total
Male	**Age 65-74**		**Age 75-84**		**Age 85 up**	
Heart Disease	1178.9	34.9%	2754.1	36.8%	7157.6	40.3%
Cancer	1111.1	32.9%	1882.8	25.2%	2802.7	15.8%
Stroke	155.8	4.6%	509.7	6.8%	1500.8	8.5%
COPD[1]	199.7	5.9%	478.6	6.4%	830.9	4.7%
Pneumonia/Flu	74.1	2.2%	310.4	4.1%	1310.4	7.4%
Diabetes	78.5	2.3%	150.9	2.0%	268.7	1.5%
Accidents	61.1	1.8%	130.8	1.7%	344.3	1.9%
Top Seven Causes	2859.2	84.7%	6217.3	83.1%	14215.4	80.1%
Total Death Rate	3374		7483		17740	
Ratio to All Ages:[2]	3.7		8.3		19.7	
Female	**Age 65-74**		**Age 75-84**		**Age 85 up**	
Heart Disease	587.8	29.8%	1776.1	37.5%	6264.0	45.1%
Cancer	686.5	34.8%	1025.6	21.7%	1394.1	10.0%
Stroke	119.2	6.0%	442.8	9.4%	1591.3	11.4%
COPD	120.7	6.1%	233.4	4.9%	317.6	2.3%
Pneumonia/Flu	40.5	2.1%	176.1	3.7%	911.3	6.6%
Diabetes	73.5	3.7%	138.0	2.9%	248.0	1.8%
Accidents	31.0	1.6%	75.3	1.6%	220.2	1.6%
Top Seven Causes	1659.2	84.2%	6217.3	81.7%	10946.5	78.7%
Total Death Rate	1971		4731		13901	
Ratio to All Ages:	2.4		5.9		17.2	
Male/Female Ratio	**Age 65-74**		**Age 75-84**		**Age 85 up**	
Heart Disease	2.01	1.17	1.55	0.98	1.14	0.90
Cancer	1.62	0.95	1.84	1.16	2.01	1.58
Stroke	1.31	0.76	1.15	0.73	0.94	0.74
COPD	1.65	0.97	2.05	1.30	2.62	2.05
Pneumonia/Flu	1.83	1.07	1.76	1.11	1.44	1.13
Diabetes	1.07	0.62	1.09	0.69	1.08	0.85
Accidents	1.97	1.15	1.74	1.10	1.56	1.23
Top Seven Causes	1.72	1.01	1.61	1.02	1.30	1.02
Total Death Rate	1.71		1.58		1.28	
Ratio of All Ages:	1.12		1.12		1.12	

1--COPD (chronic obstructive pulmonary diseases) includes bronchitis, emphysema, and asthma.

2--Ratio to All Ages is the ratio of the total death rate for the age group being considered to the overall death rate for all ages. The overall death rate for males is 901.6 and in this case the total death rate for the Age 65-74 group is 3.7 times higher than that of the overall rate.

Table 5-5 shows the key things to do to avoid premature death. Many books have been written about how to be healthy and live a long life, but detailed discussions about the various proposals are beyond the scope of this book. However, there are some basic things everyone can do that are within the control of each of us. These things are listed in Table 5-5. The concept is that by age 30 everyone has entered a period of decline in the efficiency of nearly all systems in the body. But we have large reserves, and if the rate of decline is slow enough, we can stay healthy for a long time. All of us have a great deal of control over that rate of decline. Doing just the five things listed in Table 5-5 will substantially reduce the rate of decline, and permit most of us to reach age 85, the apparent maximum average life span for the species.

Table 5-5. Preventing Premature Death

1. Do not smoke or quit now if you already do smoke.
2. Do not abuse drugs or alcohol or practice unsafe sex.
3. Maintain a desirable weight by eating appropriate foods and exercising.
4. Eat foods low in saturated fat, cholesterol, and sodium.
5. Do aerobic exercise three times a week for at least 30 minutes each time.

The first step should be no surprise to anyone who has read the preceding four parts of the book. Smoking is estimated to cause 20 percent of all deaths in the United States, including 90 percent of all deaths from lung cancer. The bad effects of smoking are one of the few things related to health that doctors agree upon, and they have demonstrated that agreement in a significant way. When the first Surgeon General's report on smoking came out in 1964, 42 percent of American adults smoked. Thirty years later only 25 percent smoked. But doctors had a more impressive change. In 1960 a huge 79 percent of all doctors smoked. By 1995 only 3.3 percent were still smoking.

You can find doctors who are overweight, who are careless about what they eat, and who don't exercise. But you will have a very hard time today finding a doctor who smokes. Doctors live with the causes and effects of disease. If nearly all of them have stopped smoking, it's a clear sign they've found the end results of the habit decidedly unpleasant. If you want to stay healthy, you should follow their unmistakable (even if perhaps unintentional) lead.

Drug and alcohol abuse damages every system in the body. Dirty needles and unsafe sex are the main methods for transmitting HIV/AIDS, the leading cause of death in males in the 25-44 age bracket (Table 5-2). These behaviors are incompatible with a long and healthy life.

The third step is important on its own because being overweight is a risk factor in premature death. But it also represents a simple indicator about how well you are doing everything else required to avoid premature death. Tables 5-6 and 5-7 offer two different ways to determine a desirable weight for your gender and height. Because maintaining a desirable weight is so hard to do, if you do it you don't need to track the results of the remaining steps in Table 5-5.

This is not to say that the remaining steps in Table 5-5 are not important. On the contrary, if you follow the first two steps (avoiding suicide on the installment plan), steps four and five are the keys to living your full life span. But it is not always easy to know if you are doing what needs to be done in steps four and five. That is why step three becomes such a good indicator. If you pay attention to what you eat, and exercise regularly in any reasonable way, you can judge your condition by the simple step of weighing yourself. If you are maintaining a desirable weight, you can be almost certain that your diet and exercise program are exactly what you need to be healthy.

Scenarios can be imagined in which a person can have a desirable weight and still not be healthy (very heavy smoking is one way to do it). But if you are following steps one and two, it is nearly impossible to have a poor diet and/or a poor exercise program and still maintain a desirable weight. Even people who are anorectic won't meet the requirement because they will not have a desirable weight, even if they are among the few who are too thin rather than too heavy. If you take reasonable steps to eat desirable foods and exercise, your scale and Table 5-6 or 5-7 will tell you if you are maintaining a desirable lifestyle.

The steps in Table 5-5 are not just speculation. A number of studies have been made to confirm that certain lifestyle habits correlate with longer life expectancy. For example, a study of 5,231 Mormon priests who followed the Mormon life style (similar to Table 5-5) showed an average life expectancy of 86.5 years at birth, well above the 73.2 years for white males in Table 1-1. The life expectancies of the priests at ages 65 and 85 were 68 percent and 79 percent higher respectively than those of the general population. A study of 10,224 men and 3,120 women in Dallas who were chosen on the basis of high physical fitness and lifestyles reflecting Table 5-5 showed similar results. Making the proper lifestyle choices will definitely produce a longer life and the avoidance of premature death. For many decades there has been little doubt among experts about what steps to take to have a healthy lifestyle. The problem is that it is hard for most people to take those steps (if it was easy to do everybody would do it).

The succeeding tables show how to do it in a relatively simple way, if you are willing to make the appropriate effort. It will not be easy to do, but by using your desirable weight as an indicator you will be able to get instant feedback on your progress. Such feedback is often the key to doing something with the intensity needed to make it a success.

Table 5-6 shows desirable weights based on recommendations from the Metropolitan Life Insurance Company. Weights are in pounds without clothes, and heights are in inches without shoes. For a man, shoes add about one inch in height, and standard indoor clothing including shoes adds about four pounds. For a woman, the added height with shoes depends on the size of the heel. Standard indoor clothing including shoes adds about three or four pounds.

The most widely accepted tables for desirable weights were issued by the Metropolitan Insurance Company in 1959. It was emphasized that the tables were not average weights, because the average person was overweight even then. The desirable weights published were those consistent with the longest life of their policy holders. Life insurance companies have a compelling interest in having their policy holders live as long as possible, so when they issue desirable weight tables it can be safely assumed the data is accurate.

In recent decades the Metropolitan Insurance Company issued new tables which added several pounds to the older tables. This was partly due to pressure from sources using the tables who wanted them to be a little easier to achieve, and partly due to data which indicated one could be too thin as well as too heavy for good health. But more recent data indicate there is effectively no such thing as being too thin. The problem is that many people who are "too thin" are in that condition because of illness or poor nutrition. Such people understandably have shorter life spans than expected. Those who are thin but who are in good health with nutritionally sound diets have the lowest mortality rates among the general population.

Thus, Table 5-6 is based on the 1959 data. A weight goal should be selected based on gender and body size (small, medium, or large). But an exact definition of body size is not critical. Many people will be above the highest weight shown for a specific height regardless of their body size. If you reduce your weight below the highest weight shown for a given height, you will be well on the way to achieving good health.

For example, if you are a woman five feet, three inches tall in bare feet, your desirable weight ranges from 107 pounds at the low end of the small frame category to 138 pounds at the high end of the large frame category. If you weigh more than 138 pounds, the first goal is to reduce to that level without any regard for your estimated frame size. Once you are below 138 pounds, moving down to a level consistent with your estimated frame size will improve your health, but staying permanently below 138 pounds will insure you are gaining much of the benefits of weight reduction.

Table 5-7 shows a relatively new technique for determining desirable weights that eliminates the problem of determining frame size. It also is considered more useful for the purpose, because it focuses on the level of body fat which is the key issue in weight reduction.

Table 5-6. Recommended Weight by Height

Height	Small	Size of Frame (Male) Medium	Large
Five feet, one inch	105-113	111-122	119-134
Five feet, two inches	108-116	114-126	122-137
Five feet, three inches	111-119	117-129	125-141
Five feet, four inches	114-122	120-132	128-145
Five feet, five inches	117-126	123-136	131-149
Five feet, six inches	121-130	127-140	135-154
Five feet, seven inches	125-134	131-145	140-159
Five feet, eight inches	129-138	135-149	144-163
Five feet, nine inches	133-143	139-153	148-167
Five feet, ten inches	137-147	143-158	152-172
Five feet, eleven inches	141-151	147-163	156-177
Six feet	145-155	151-168	161-182
Six feet, one inch	149-160	155-173	166-187
Six feet, two inches	153-164	160-178	171-192
Six feet, three inches	157-168	165-183	175-197

Height	Small	Size of Frame (Female) Medium	Large
Four feet, eight inches	88-94	92-103	100-114
Four feet, nine inches	90-97	94-106	102-118
Four feet, ten inches	92-100	97-109	105-121
Four feet, eleven inches	95-103	100-112	108-124
Five feet	98-106	103-115	111-127
Five feet, one inch	101-109	106-118	114-130
Five feet, two inches	104-112	109-122	117-134
Five feet, three inches	107-115	112-126	121-138
Five feet, four inches	110-119	116-131	125-142
Five feet, five inches	114-123	120-135	129-146
Five feet, six inches	118-127	124-139	133-150
Five feet, seven inches	122-131	128-143	137-154
Five feet, eight inches	126-136	132-147	141-159
Five feet, nine inches	130-140	136-151	145-164
Five feet, ten inches	134-144	140-155	149-169

Note: Height is without shoes and weight is in pounds without clothes.

Table 5-7 shows desirable weights for both men and women using the relatively new concept of Body Mass Index (BMI). BMI is a good indicator of the level of body fat, the key issue in weight reduction. It is determined by multiplying weight in pounds by 700 and dividing by the square of height in inches. The result is compared to standards adopted by the National Health and Nutrition Examination Survey. Once again, weights are in pounds without clothes and heights are in inches without shoes. Table 5-6 shows estimates for correcting for the addition of shoes and clothes.

The BMI values are in bold type at the top of the two sections of Table 5-7. The top section of the table includes BMI values from 19 through 25. These are the BMI values consistent with good health. A BMI level above 25 is on the borderline of the official definition of obesity, even though the average level in the general population is 23 for women and 24 for men. The best goal for most people is a BMI value in the 21-22 range, although the lower the BMI value the lower the mortality rate, even down to levels below 19.

The bottom section of Table 5-7 includes BMI values from 26 through 32. Readings in the 27-28 range are officially defined as obese, and readings above 31-32 are very obese. Persons with a BMI level above 31 should see a doctor because their health is at risk. Defining desirable BMI levels is based on data comparing mortality levels for people with different BMI levels. Any person with a BMI level above a baseline of 21 has an increased risk of mortality. For example, people with BMI levels of 30 have a 50 percent higher mortality rate than persons with BMI levels of 21.

Comparing Tables 5-6 and 5-7 shows that the desired weights for a given height in Table 5-6 are close to the weights that give a BMI reading of 21-22. For example, a man with a medium frame who is five feet, seven inches tall in his bare feet has a desirable weight of 138 pounds in Table 5-6 (midway between the 131 and 145 pound limits). Table 5-7 shows that a weight of 138 pounds with a height of five feet, seven inches corresponds to a BMI of about 21.5. A woman in the same category has a desirable weight of 135 in Table 5-6 which corresponds to a BMI value of 21 in Table 5-7.

Another measure indicative of good health that ties to BMI is the ratio of waist size to hip size. BMI indicates how much body fat a person has, and the ratio indicates where the fat is located. The maximum desired ratio is 1.0 for men and 0.8 for women. In each case, the lower the ratio the better. For example, men with ratios above 1.0 have twice the death rate from heart attack and stroke as do men who have ratios of 0.85. But if you achieve BMI values near 21-22, you can expect desirable waist-to-hip ratios nearly automatically.

Achieving desirable weights is not easy, but many people have very stable weights 30-40 pounds above the desirable level. Table 5-8 shows how to get rid of those extra pounds in a year with surprisingly few changes in lifestyle.

Table 5-7. Body Mass Index by Height

Height Without Shoes   Weight Without Clothes (pounds)

Body Mass Index	19	20	21	22	23	24	25
Four feet, eight inches	85	90	94	99	103	108	112
Four feet, nine inches	88	93	97	102	107	111	116
Four feet, ten inches	91	96	101	106	111	115	120
Four feet, eleven inches	94	99	104	109	114	119	124
Five feet	98	103	108	113	118	123	129
Five feet, one inch	101	106	112	117	122	128	133
Five feet, two inches	104	110	115	121	126	132	137
Five feet, three inches	108	113	119	125	130	136	142
Five feet, four inches	111	117	123	129	135	140	146
Five feet, five inches	115	121	127	133	139	145	151
Five feet, six inches	118	124	131	137	143	149	156
Five feet, seven inches	122	128	135	141	147	154	160
Five feet, eight inches	126	132	139	145	152	159	165
Five feet, nine inches	129	136	143	150	156	163	170
Five feet, ten inches	133	140	147	154	161	168	175
Five feet, eleven inches	137	144	151	158	166	173	180
Six feet	141	148	156	163	170	178	185
Six feet, one inch	145	152	160	167	175	183	190
Six feet, two inches	149	156	164	172	180	188	196
Six feet, three inches	153	161	169	177	185	193	201

Body Mass Index	26	27	28	29	30	31	32
Four feet, eight inches	116	121	125	130	134	139	143
Four feet, nine inches	121	125	130	135	139	144	149
Four feet, ten inches	125	130	135	139	144	149	154
Four feet, eleven inches	129	134	139	144	149	154	159
Five feet	134	139	144	149	154	159	165
Five feet, one inch	138	144	149	154	159	165	170
Five feet, two inches	143	148	154	159	165	170	176
Five feet, three inches	147	153	159	164	170	176	181
Five feet, four inches	152	158	164	170	176	181	187
Five feet, five inches	157	163	169	175	181	187	193
Five feet, six inches	162	168	174	180	187	193	199
Five feet, seven inches	167	173	180	186	192	199	205
Five feet, eight inches	172	178	185	192	198	205	211
Five feet, nine inches	177	184	190	197	204	211	218
Five feet, ten inches	182	189	196	203	210	217	224
Five feet, eleven inches	187	194	202	209	216	223	230
Six feet	193	200	207	215	222	230	237
Six feet, one inch	198	206	213	221	228	236	244
Six feet, two inches	203	211	219	227	235	243	250
Six feet, three inches	209	217	225	233	241	249	257

Table 5-8 shows the number of pounds that can be lost in one year by eliminating food items consumed every day. The table shows items by category, the number of ounces in the typical serving listed, the number of calories in the ounces shown, and the total pounds lost in one year if the items are eliminated (assuming they were previously eaten every day).

The results of Table 5-8 can be applied to any food item by a simple rule of thumb. When the body receives more calories than it needs, the excess is stored as fat. A pound of fat represents about 3800 calories. With 365 days in a year, a little over 10 calories a day accounts for a pound of fat. Thus, if the number of calories in a serving of food is divided by 10, the result is the number of pounds the serving represents in a year if consumed every day. Eating or drinking more than the serving shown in Table 5-8 directly multiplies the effect. Thus, while drinking one soft drink every day adds 14 pounds in a year, drinking a size 50 percent bigger than the 12 ounces shown means a 50 percent increase in pounds. Many of us eat or drink certain items every day without realizing how many pounds they contribute to our weight over a full year.

The first category in Table 5-8 is beverages because it is easier to drink excess calories than to eat them. Someone consuming a small glass of dessert wine with dinner every day will probably be shocked to find it adds 25 pounds in a year. Eliminating the wine will produce a loss of 25 pounds in one year without changing anything else in the diet or doing another minute of exercise. Similarly, many people drink soft drinks daily without realizing the added weight they produce. Switching to sugar free drinks would save lots of pounds.

Selecting items from the other categories produces similar surprising results. Eating one large candy bar every day for a snack adds an astounding 49 pounds in a year. The pastries that often go with coffee breaks represent from 20 to 40 pounds in a year. Those chocolate covered ice cream cones from the freezer represent 34 pounds. The typical combinations shown at the bottom of Table 5-8 offer even quicker weight loss results. For example, many people eat the first combination of a soft drink, potato chips, and three small cookies in addition to their regular lunch. Dropping these lunch additives drops 45 pounds in a year. Even if they are consumed only five days a week with lunch at work, the resulting weight loss is five-sevenths of the total or 32 pounds a year. Substantial reductions of weight are closer at hand than most of us realize.

Another advantage of eliminating the items shown in Table 5-8 is that not only do they contribute to weight loss, they also reduce the amount of saturated fat, cholesterol, sugar, and salt in the daily diet. These are the four things most harmful to good health in normal diets. If the reduction of these items in the diet is added to one of the simple exercise plans shown in Table 5-9, the result is both weight loss and the achievement of the good health needed to avoid premature death.

Table 5-8. One Year Weight Effects from Daily Intakes

Item	Ounces Per Serving	Calories	Pounds Per Year
Beverages			
Cola soft drink, regular size	12.0	140	14
Fruit soft drink, regular size	12.0	210	21
Standard beer, regular size	12.0	140	14
Hard liquor, one jigger	1.5	110	11
Dessert wine, small glass	6.0	250	25
Dry wine, small glass	6.0	130	13
Snacks			
Candy bar, regular size	2.0	280	28
Candy bar, large size	3.5	490	49
Hard candy, six pieces	1.3	140	14
Potato chips, one small bag	1.0	150	15
Baked Goods			
Cookies, three small chocolate chip	1.1	160	16
Doughnut, one full size	2.1	280	28
Doughnut, one small sugar type	1.4	190	19
Pastry, one bear claw type	2.3	270	27
Cinnamon roll, small	1.4	140	14
Cinnamon roll, large	4.0	380	38
Apple strudel, one regular piece	2.7	270	27
Dairy Products			
Frozen ice cream cone with toppings	3.8	340	34
Regular ice cream, two dips	2.4	140	14
Typical Combinations			
Cola soft drink	12.0	140	14
Small bag of potato chips	1.0	150	15
Three small chocolate chip cookies	1.1	160	16
Total weight gain per year: 45 pounds			
Cola soft drink	12.0	140	14
One full size doughnut	2.1	280	28
Total weight gain per year: 42 pounds			
Large candy bar	3.5	490	49
Six pieces hard candy	1.3	140	14
Total weight gain per year: 63 pounds			

Table 5-9 shows the key aspects of exercise. Part I shows the weight loss that results from taking part in different activities three hours each week at various levels of intensity. Part II shows the heart rates necessary during exercise to permit a reduction in the number of hours of exercise per week while still maintaining its key benefits. Part III lists the key benefits of exercise that accrue in addition to weight loss.

Part I shows that the more intensive the exercise the more weight lost for the same duration of exercise. Alternatively, you can lose the same weight at a lower level of intensity if you exercise longer. The same amount of weight is lost whether you run a mile or walk a mile. But it takes longer to walk a mile than to run a mile. If you have lots of time, you can lose weight at low levels of intensity. If you are pressed for time, increasing the intensity gains the benefit in less time. For example, walking at 3 miles per hour (about the maximum speed at which people can walk) for 3 hours a week produces a weight loss of 12 pounds a year. If you jog at 5 miles per hour (anything faster is running) for 3 hours a week, you will lose 20 pounds a year. If you jogged at 5 miles per hour for only 1.8 hours per week, you would lose the same 12 pounds lost by walking 3 miles per hour for 3 hours.

Part II shows the heart rate required to get the maximum benefits of exercise for the systems in your body. In Part I, any amount of total exercise will produce a weight loss if performed for a long enough time. But to improve significantly the systems in your body, you need to keep your heart at a specific percentage of its maximum rate for at least 30 minutes each time three times a week (1.5 hours total). Exercising at the 75-80 percent level is the goal. This level of intensity roughly corresponds to activities/intensities that produce a weight loss of more than 16 pounds in Part I. But you must be in good physical shape before exercising at the 75-80 percent level. It's best to start at 60 percent and slowly work your way up, and exercising near or above 85 percent is dangerous. If you exercise three hours per week at the 75-80 percent level, you are getting all the benefits exercise has to offer. There are no additional benefits to be gained by exercising longer than three hours at this level of intensity.

Part III shows the key benefits of exercise. These actually are the primary reasons for exercising. Weight loss is just a pleasant side effect. If you do not smoke, do not abuse drugs and alcohol, and do not practice unsafe sex, then realizing through exercise the key benefits listed in Part III is the most important thing you can do to avoid premature death. If you exercise at the intensity levels outlined in Part II, you will find it nearly impossible to be overweight. Weight loss is helpful in preventing premature death, and controlling your weight is a simple and excellent indicator of the state of your health, as outlined in the text accompanying Table 5-5. But if you had to pick just one thing to concentrate on, exercise would be it.

Table 5-9. Key Aspects of Exercise

Part I: Yearly Weight Loss for Three Hours of Exercise per Week

Pounds Lost per Year:	6	8	12	16	20	30
Walking/running, miles per hour	1	2	3	4	5	7
Bicycle riding, miles per hour		5	6	10	12	14
Aerobics (level of effort)				Low	Medium	High
Golf[1]			Ride[1]	Cart	Carry	
Tennis, competitive play				Doubles	Singles	

1--"Ride" is a motorized cart; "Cart" is pulling a bag cart; "Carry" is carrying your clubs.

Part II: Heart Rates to Gain Full Benefits of Exercise in 1.5 Hours per Week

Percent of Maximum:	60%	70%	75%	80%	85%
Age Maximum					
20 200	120	140	150	160	170
25 195	117	137	146	156	166
30 190	114	133	143	152	162
35 185	111	130	139	148	157
40 180	108	126	135	144	153
45 175	105	123	131	140	149
50 170	102	119	128	136	145
55 165	99	116	124	132	140
60 160	96	112	120	128	136
65 155	93	109	116	124	132
70 150	90	105	113	120	128
75 145	87	102	109	116	123
80 140	84	98	105	112	119

Part III: Key Benefits of Any Level of Exercise

1. Improves cardiac and pulmonary reserve.
2. Reduces blood clotting risks.
3. Increases high-density lipoproteins (HDL) and improves the serum cholesterol ratio in the blood.
4. Helps control weight.
5. Adds bone and muscle strength and improves bowel function.
6. Improves glucose utilization.
7. Increases maximal oxygen intake. This item may be the most critical. When the maximal oxygen uptake drops below the minimal requirements of the body, even in the absence of disease, the result is death. This is essentially the definition of death from old age.

Index